it begins
it ends
it ends
it begins

D1158029

paul reps

letters to a friend   writings & drawings   1939 to 1980

stillgate publishers   south acworth   new hampshire

This "Reps spasm you are effulging" (as Paul Reps describes it) has been compiled from the eclectic assortment of letters, postcards, manuscripts, brush drawings and newspaper clippings which Reps has mailed his friend Bill over the last 30 years. All of the text and art in this book is taken from either these mailings or from previously published Reps work.

This is the first published collection of Reps' letters, and it includes the first reproduction of his drawings on soft Japanese paper in twenty years. This type of paper, made primarily from mulberry bark (kozo) is the original medium for Reps' finest work. These reproductions are, therefore, the only true reproductions.

The production of this book was inspired and guided by the advice, encouragement, cajoling and insight of both Reps and Bill. Many other people have provided invaluable assistance, enthusiasm and energy of all kinds. We are grateful.

Stillgate Publishers

Art Credits

Designed by Stillgate Publishers; Typesetting by Donald Bustin and Trade Composition; Mechanical art by Marcie Dreyer and Diane Gearhart.

Photography Credits

p. 2 — Robert James; pp. 8, 9, 76 — Ira Gavrin; pp. 72, 95 — Mark Semon; pp. 73, 161 and throughout Chapter 3 — Hyam Siegel.

Magazine Credits

Material on p. 77 © 1957 Mainichi Daily News; p. 78 © 1967 Goteborgs-Posten; p. 81 © 1967 University of Colorado Daily; pp. 41–43, 140, 141, 167, 168 © 1955 Reporter Publications, Inc.; p. 75 © 1967 by Newsweek, Inc.; All Rights Reserved. Reprinted by Permission.

Book Credits

Material on some pages first appeared in various Reps books from the following publishers: pp. 64, 65, 94, 102–104, 106–110, 113, 116, 117, 130–133 © Charles Tuttle Co.; p. 101 — Preview Publications; p. 105 — Sequoia University Press; pp. 44, 123, 124 — John Weatherhill, Inc.; pp. 125 © Zen Center Press; pp. 99, 126, 127 — Doubleday & Co.; pp. 111, 114 — Liu Publishers; pp. 118–121 — Doric Publishing Co. All copyrights held by Paul Reps unless otherwise indicated. All Rights Reserved. Reprinted by Permission. A complete Reps bibliography appears on page 184.

It is probable we meet only the persons in this world we deserve to meet, or are supposed to meet, or are drawn to meet, like certain water drops down a stream gliding over certain stones on their way to the sea.

Reps

LETTERS

"having spoiled
the exquisite
with my thoughts
let me spoil you
with my words."

"art is organized
and art is expensive
and the name art is separative
i'm just having a good time."

"these writings and drawings
gathered from reps' life
free me (you)
already free."

"we wake as angels, and go to sleep
as devils because we don't know
how to spend our waking day
let me tell you how!"

DRAWINGS

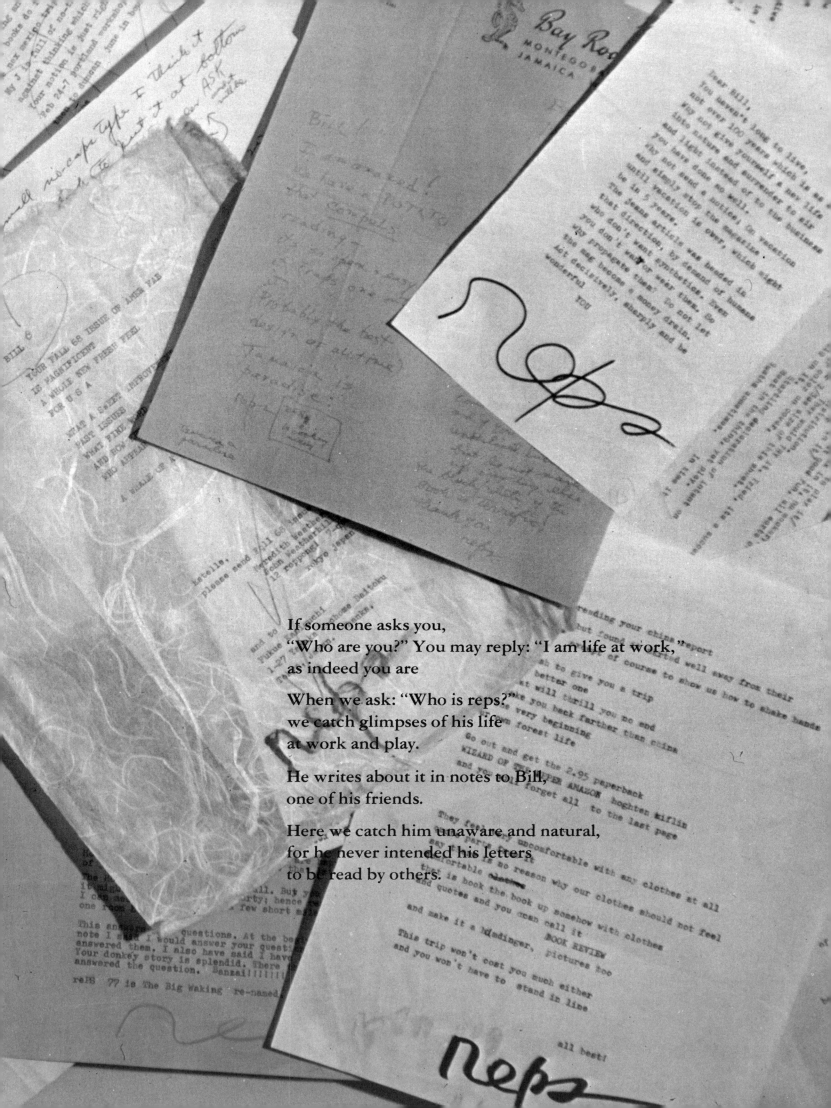

If someone asks you,
"Who are you?" You may reply: "I am life at work,"
as indeed you are

When we ask: "Who is reps?"
we catch glimpses of his life
at work and play.

He writes about it in notes to Bill,
one of his friends.

Here we catch him unaware and natural,
for he never intended his letters
to be read by others.

INTRODUCTION

"Bones, not accompanied by precise information as to their spatial and temporal provenance, are not worth accepting because they cannot be used for research." *   *This book might be called "Reps Flesh Reps Bones."*

"A cucumber cucumbering" contains not one iota less meaning than "I am that I am," and Paul Reps would be the first to affirm it. Reps can be called the latest in a line of poet-philosophers extending back thousands of years. He is, by all criteria, one of the most modern and inventive voices proclaiming, "Isness is . . . always and no matter what."

FIRST
MEETING

I meet Reps a few years after the end of World War II. He has been writing travel stories for *AFF* and *Gentry* magazines, which I publish at the time, and in one of his notes to me accompanying an article, he mentions that he is going to Japan and proposes that I make the trip with him, if I can arrange it. He will meet me in Los Angeles and will carry a small knapsack with an identifying red rose pinned onto it.

The flight from New York takes almost three days, with stopovers or connections in Los Angeles, Honolulu, and Wake Island. When I arrive at the old Spanish Colonial style airport in L.A., I find Reps waiting at the arrival gate, all dressed up in a pair of chino pants and shirt, carrying the small rose-bedecked knapsack. I know the secret of traveling light, but here he is, setting out on a three-months-or-more trip to the Orient, with a miniscule backpack containing only books and writing materials. This is my first face-to-face meeting with him.

Our first stop is Honolulu which, along with the rest of Hawaii,

*W.C. Sturtevant, Anthropologist, Smithsonian Institution.

is still relatively unspoiled by tourism and industrialization. We stay at the home of a former U.S. Army Captain, an old friend of mine, who has settled there with his Japanese wife. Before long Mr. and Mrs. Army Captain and their year-old baby succumb completely to Reps' charm. When we depart a few days later, he leaves behind some dozen poems written especially for the child.

Our prop plane is full of military personnel and their families, and returning Japanese. A wondrous picture-landscape looms before our eyes as we catch our first glimpse of Tokyo. Tokyo Bay sparkles clearly in the distance. The small harbor is surrounded by clusters of fishing dwellings.

Entry formalities are uncomplicated for foreigners and, a few minutes after we touch land, Reps, relatively unknown in the United States, is being greeted by a group of some forty admirers, including several poets and publishers, who escort us into the city. This first welcome is a mere hint of the warm hospitality which is to come: receptions and dinners inundate us for the first few weeks.

One of the first of these dinners is given for Reps by the Ambassador of India. The speeches begin to get boring. Suddenly, Reps gets up and signals to me saying: "Let's go." To the astonishment of the gaping crowd we exit.

Just as he is a great get-upper and leaver, he is also a great let's-goer. In the middle of a poetry reading one evening our friend Tokuzawa speaks about a seeress who lives on a mountain several hundreds of miles to the south. Reps says immediately: "Let's go." "Tomorrow, you mean?" I ask. "No," he says, "we leave right now." Tokuzawa and I look at each other. Sure enough, the three of us head for the Central Tokyo railway station and wait there for the first train connection in the direction of Miyako-jima.

After several train and bus rides we find ourselves on a ferry, crossing towards a mountainous island in the Japan Sea. Upon landing we start a two-hour climb up a steep mountainside. At the top is a clearing with a small hut. As we approach, a bright-eyed smiling

THE
SEERESS

old lady emerges to greet us, trailed by a boy about 12 years old.

The old lady, according to Tokuzawa, our interpreter, is some 90 years old, and has lived on the mountain for the last 50 or 60 years. Her disciples and followers, mostly fishermen and farmers in the area, bring her food and other necessities. Winter and summer, spring and fall, she lives on the top of this mountain, rarely coming down to the village on the mainland.

The boy, who is her attendant, never speaks. He is a deaf-mute foundling. We can not help observing over the next few days the touching relationship between the old lady and the boy.

During our visit she shows us a cave which has been carved out of the solid rock. To reach the cave, we have to walk on a narrow ledge. The old lady assures us that it is safe. We follow her, she supported by her cane, we by our faith in her assurances. As we sit in the cave, she tells us that she has, with her own hands, built the path and transformed the cave into a habitable dwelling.

"I lived here for more than forty years before the hut was built."

"Weren't you afraid to be here all alone?"

"No, no . . . but yes, sometimes when there was a storm, when lightning bolts struck against the mountainside and the thunder crashed — in those moments I prayed with extra strength."

Many of the local populace regard her as a prophetess. One morning we see two ravens fly to her when she whistles and remain motionless while she ties small pieces of paper to their necks. At a signal they fly off down through the clouds. She tells us that she uses the ravens to carry messages to her followers on the mainland.

Arising early one morning before our departure, I see a fire in the clearing before the hut. Around the fire the deaf-mute boy is dancing and chanting, his voice clear and beautiful.

When we leave for the climb down to the ferry landing, she gives us her farewell blessing. Several hours later, turning onto the bustling main street of the nearby Japanese town, there in the crowd we spot the seeress, attended by the boy. How the two got down the mountain before us, we do not know.

On his periodic visits to Japan, Reps visits Soen Nakagawa, the Zen head of Ryutakuji, in Mishima City. As a mark of his esteem and special affection, Soen (who looks on Reps as one of the most original poets of our times) places at his disposal a small hut outside the monastery gates. Here Reps occupies himself with his writing.

One morning I stroll over to this lodging and find him jubilantly waving a sheet of paper. He has just completed a new three-word poem. I extend my congratulations and we both agree that it is the greatest minimal bit of verse he has ever written.

That morning, as the winter sun brightens, we go off for a walk, soon finding ourselves on a hill overlooking the local cemetery. Protected from the wind, we strip to enjoy a welcome sunbath. As the morning lengthens and becomes warmer, we doze off. Sleepily, I say to Reps: "That was a fine poem you wrote this morning, please recite it again." He looks at me, scratches his head and exclaims: "I have forgotten it!" I have forgotten it too. We burst into laughter, rolling on the ground, at the idea that neither of us can remember the three words of the best poem he ever has written.

That very night we accompany Soen to a big dinner at the home of a rich neighboring farmer. From time to time the monks are treated to a lavish meal by one or another of the local gentry. Soen, particularly concerned with the appearance as well as the decorum of his monks, lines us up in front of the zendo for inspection. He produces two *hakama* (trousers), one for Paul and one for myself, and after much arranging and re-arranging, he declares us acceptable members of the retinue. The night is lit by a full moon and we walk about 2 or 3 miles across the countryside passing through several villages on our way. We move to the measured beat of the drum, our passage along the narrow dikes further lit up by torches carried by several monks.

The farm house is old-fashioned with a large interior courtyard occupied by horses, cows, and pigs. The feast begins and ends with hot sake served in soup bowls. Ravishingly hungry, because of prolonged monastery diets, the monks go at it with gusto. Bowl after bowl of sake is downed and immense dishes of food are consumed. After the feast there is chanting, and there are prayers in honor of the dead relatives of our farmer host. The chanting, while a bit uneven, has a tone not too different from what we are accustomed to hearing in the monastery. Still, it is different enough to encourage Paul and me to join the chorus, mingling our voices with the Buddhists, much to the astonishment and murmured approval of the farmer and his family.

As we stagger back to the monastery, we continue our chanting. The beat of the drum is louder and richer than ever. The torches flicker like huge fireflies in the wind. Even Soen himself agrees it has been a glorious evening.

R.H. BLYTH AND THE ABSOLUTE

Reps is always an appreciative admirer of other writers. He suggests we visit R.H. Blyth, the author of *Zen in English Literature and Oriental Classics,* and of a series of books on haiku. Transportation is difficult around the Tokyo area, and we have to make a rather circuitous journey to arrive at Blyth's home. There we are greeted with expansive hospitality. Though Reps is seldom at a loss for words, and quite adept at holding the center of the conversational stage, this is one occasion where he never gets off the ground. He seems to take pleasure in the polished eloquence of the English writer.

While the discussion touches on the Absolute and the Relative, as well as on the relative-absolute, I myself have a vivid memory of Mrs. Blyth, a Japanese lady of great beauty and distinction, who joins the conversation from time to time.

REPS AND THE ROCK

Reps' gamut of admirers ranges from infants to intellectuals, and among them is Susumu Ijiri, the relatively unknown founder of a system which combines Sufism and Buddhism. We spend a few days at Ijiri's center near the City of Himeji in Hyogo Prefecture. There

Reps first sees, and later reports on, the four-sides-and-center pillow game which is used in the education of children. **

A large meditation stone, known as the "Reps Rock," has been laboriously moved up to the top of the hill overlooking the commune in preparation for our visit. It is touching to see the affection and the care which Ijiri's followers give to the rock. Equally touching is Paul's whole-hearted response to everyone there, be they the least of Ijiri's followers or the youngest of the children.

LOSING ONE'S VIRTUE

I have letters of introduction from Dr. D.T. Suzuki to several Zen masters and I am anxious to use them. Finally, after five or six weeks of traveling with Paul, I tell him I am heading for Eiheiji, a monastery in Western Japan, where I intend to stay for a period of time. His reaction is typical: "Please, don't shut yourself in a monastery, they'll spoil you."

I take this not so much as a compliment to my pristine virtue, but rather as his wish not to lose a traveling companion. Still, by and large, Reps is a loner. He likes to be by himself, and indeed for long periods he is by himself.

DANCING GIRLS AND BUDDHA

One day Reps announces that we are invited on a road tour with a theatrical company. We are at the railroad station the next day with about a hundred young Japanese girls who are the dancers of the troupe. The Japanese railroads are being rebuilt at this time and there are no sleeping coaches. We are often compelled to travel sitting up at night in order to arrive on time for the next performance.

Reps' friend, the director and choreographer, is also the chief actor, taking the title role in *The Life of Buddha*. Before each performance the director-friend declaims a few of Reps' verses in Japanese, always with a grand flourish towards where the poet is sitting. It all ends abruptly, alas, when Paul announces with a grin: "No more Buddha-loving to Reps."

**Essentially, this is a game where the child learns to see points of view other than his or her own. The Reps article appeared in *The Mainichi*, October 27, 1958, and was later reprinted in *Square Sun Square Moon*.

My own activities send me regularly to the Orient. As often as I can, usually on my way home, I call on Reps, who has, for a long time, spent a good part of each year in Japan and Hawaii. At this time Reps is living on the big island of Hawaii, near the village of Paauilo. Here he has built a small dwelling place with a roof open to the sky. He is deeply into ecology. He always has been finicky about the air he breathes and the food he eats, very finicky for a man who professes total belief in *Self*. But on this occasion he does depart radically from his essential vegetarian diet.

It is a day or two after I arrive when he announces that he has a special treat for me: "Bill, I have found an extraordinary river where you simply jump in and the current takes you for a good distance downstream and deposits you at a safe landing."

Off we go, coming to a wide meandering stream which flows in a deep ravine. Taking our clothes off, we jump in. Sure enough, the current behaves exactly as he promised. By letting ourselves float, we are borne rapidly but gently with the current and land about three-quarters of a mile downstream on a safe sand bar. It is fun, so we walk back to try again.

But now the current has changed. It is much swifter, much more turbulent. Nevertheless, Reps jumps in. In a moment or two I see that he is in serious difficulty. Waving to me he shouts: "Don't come in . . . wait . . . wait . . ." I run along the bank as he makes efforts to swim against the drag of the current. But the strength and the direction of the river course has changed. Being a fair swimmer I jump in, trying to help, but it is obvious immediately that I can not do very much. Finally, with some luck, we manage to pull ourselves out of the river's grip and are able to reach land, exhausted by our efforts.

Finding our way to the nearest road, we are finally picked up by a passing farmer, who takes us in his truck to the local tavern. Reps immediately orders whiskey and broiled steak. Noting my questioning look at this deviation from his vegetarian diet he mutters: "Sometimes when depleted of energy, a man needs some red meat and a stiff drink."

Several years later, he sends me a local clipping which speaks about the "Revenging River" — it is, of course, the very one where we almost lost our lives.

Watching Reps work is an experience itself. On his small portable typewriter he types a dozen or more drafts of what he intends to say. For a six-line verse he may do literally a score of drafts before he accepts the final one. The spare sentences, the simple poems he writes, are the polished result of a hard working craftsman. These published letters, however, are first drafts — quickly, spontaneously written — and so have their own special flavor, different from his more formal literary efforts.

About his well known adaptations of Nyogen Senzaki's original translation from the Chinese of *The Gateless Gate, 10 Bulls,* and *101 Zen Stories*†, Mary Farkas, of the First Zen Institute of America, wrote: "Though Reps did not know one Chinese character from another, he was able to 'transcribe' Senzaki's succinct and forceful literalness, to convey the essence of the original's simple structure, into a rare pure distillation of English Reps himself thought of as classic. It is a style I particularly enjoy."††

REPS AS
WRITER

The exhibits of his drawings, which have been held in various museums in Sweden, Norway, Japan, Great Britain, and Canada, as well as in the United States, are a tribute to a formidable talent. His work has also been reproduced in ceramics and textiles. From the moment he first began to work with the brush, he produced figures and lines of great vigor and depth. ‡

AND ARTIST

It is interesting to relate how he began to express himself through lines as well as in words. It seems that during his first trips to Japan, traveling to out-of-the-way small villages and towns, it was difficult to find places to eat. There were, at that time, further complications calculating the bill for the food, and making the proper payment. Reps had the habit of writing a few words of appreciation and gratitude for the meals he had been served. He would scribble a few lines on a piece of paper and hand it to the proprietor who was usually also

†Published by Charles Tuttle Co. in one volume called *Zen Flesh Zen Bones.*
††*Zen Notes,* vol. XXI, June 1974.

‡Reps says it differently. He once wrote me, "I am not an artist. I call myself an artist so that makes me one. I shape some colors like a child and name them paintings. Like other artists I price my paintings high, even $20 for twenty of them. No one buys them so I buy them myself and give them away. Sometimes I put words on them without any extra charge. What fun!"

the cook. The reception people accorded these slips of paper, written in a language they could not read, was astonishing. The restaurateurs really valued them.

After a while, Reps, disturbed at giving pieces of paper which could not be understood, began to make signs or hieroglyphics which depicted some familiar landmark of the neighborhood, or a special detail of the restaurant itself. From this beginning, Reps became more and more interested in calligraphy, developing his own original way of drawing.

ON
CENTERING

For Reps, who also transcribed Lakshmanjoo's ancient document *Centering,* ‡‡ the idea of being able to touch other worlds is more than an act of faith. It is an experience which Reps affirms to be everyone's every-moment possibility.

Like Bankei, the late 17th Century Zen Master who believed that the unborn Buddha mind is, was, always shall be, Reps insists that this mysterious timeless spaceless element exists in every creature. At the same time, the fact that the phenomenal world is unable adequately to express the world of noumena, the fact that *this* cannot comprehend *that,* does not bother him one bit. He takes Bankei's position: Don't worry — just look.

REPS'
SECRET

Despite his open-hearted generosity in sharing with everybody he meets, he is frequently accused of being overly interested in himself. Many people are put off by his odd habit of referring to himself by name: "Reps says . . . . Reps did this. . . . Reps believes. . . ." Living as he does with a moment-by-moment awareness of the Open Secret, he is innocent of egotism as we know the term. Seeing himself from *Self,* he cannot be blamed when he expresses puzzlement at such criticism. But I suppose he says to himself — who is the one who is hurt, and who is the hurter?

Whoever studies Reps' collection of writings and letters, his spe-

‡‡Centering first appeared in *Gentry Magazine,* Spring 1955, and then later in *Zen Flesh Zen Bones.* The *Gentry* version appears on pp. 41–43 of this book.

cial way of saying what the Bibles of the world have been trumpeting for thousands of years, may or may not be privy to the direct experience: the opening of oneself to oneself. At the least, his readers can rest assured that they will certainly find a lot of freshly expressed ideas in any of his books.

Like so many other gifted commentators, he keeps telling his readers that *you* are not *you* — well, you are not exactly who you think you are. He is yelling it out loudly, at the top of his eloquent voice. But the answer to "Who you?" still remains an open secret.

—W.C.S.

Glossary

[*some people and ideas you will meet in this book in the order of their appearance*]

Bill — William Segal; publisher of *American Fabrics and Fashions* and *Gentry*; recipient of the letters

Cora — his wife

Elizabeth — one of their daughters

Maharshi (Sri Ramana) — 20th c. master from India whom Reps met in the early 1900's

Dogen — 13th c. Zen master; founder of Soto sect of Zen Buddhism

Hui Neng — the 6th patriarch of Chinese Zen Buddhism

Huang Po — 9th c. Chinese Zen master

Bucky (Fuller) — contemporary American philosopher, inventor

Soen — contemporary Japanese Zen Master

Patanjali Yoga Sutras — aphorisms written by Patanjali, 3rd c. legendary founder of Yoga

Roshi Suzuki — contemporary Zen master, author of ZEN MIND BEGINNERS MIND

Baker (Richard) — successor to Suzuki Roshi

Soto — sect of Zen Buddhism; called the "gentle way"

Rinzai — sect of Zen Buddhism; called the "direct" or "sudden way"

D. T. Suzuki — 20th c. author of many books on Zen Buddhism

Hwang Ti — legendary founder of Taoism

R. H. Blyth — author of ZEN AND ZEN CLASSICS; first westerner to write extensively about Zen Buddhism

To-Lun — contemporary Buddhist abbot

Upanishads — sacred books of Vedanta, Indian philosophy

Mahesh Yogi (Maharishi) — contemporary Indian Yogi

Ram Das — contemporary Hindu Saint (not to be confused with Baba Ram Dass)

Krishnabai — his consort

Basho — 17th c. Haiku poet and Zen wanderer

Mokujiki — highly original Japanese sculptor

Appel (Karel) — contemporary Dutch painter

Rama — incarnation of Vishnu in Hindu myth; born on earth to banish the demon king Ravana

Nyogen Senzaki — Zen monk who collaborated with Reps on ZEN FLESH ZEN BONES

Liu (Jimmy) — Reps' Hong Kong publisher

Bhagavad Gita — an epic classic of Hinduism, the story of Arjuna and Krishna

Houris — beautiful maidens of Muslim paradise

Ohsawa (George) — founder of "Zen Macrobiotics," an oriental approach to diet and health

Chrow (Larry) — an American friend and fellow traveller of Reps, Bill, and many Oriental teachers

Kervran (Louis) — contemporary French alchemical scientist

Paavo Airola — nutritionist and naturopathic physician

Ramamurti Yogi (Mishra) — founder of Yoga societies in New York and San Francisco

Moshe Feldenkrais — contemporary healer; developer of technique of "Structural Integration"

W. P. Knowles — health enthusiast and proponent of breathing exercises

Ann Wigmore — natural healer; founder of Hippocrates Health Center in Boston

Marielle — Bill's second wife

Janov (Arthur) — contemporary psychotherapist; developer of "Primal Therapy"

the moment
I stop.
concepting
frees me
(of concepting).
this in itself
is the way

reps

1 instant reps

[*On Zen, Yoga, Hinduism, Buddhism, and assorted other ancient and modern gurus, religions and ways, including Centering*]

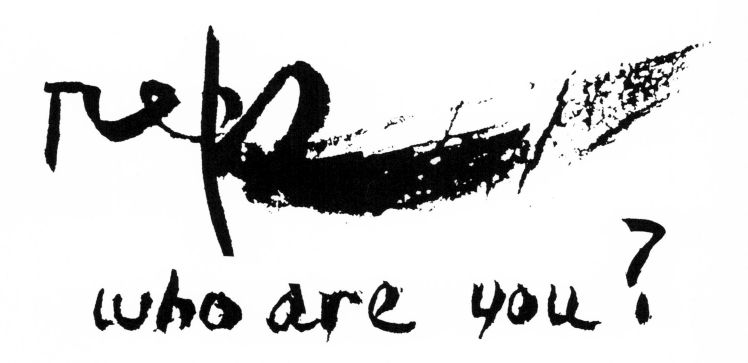

who are you?

I was born in the mid west and as soon as I got conscious I went to India. (I've been several times in India). And I've spent part of 14 years in Japan, some on the China mainland.

I have been interested all my life in the inner life. Now the outer life is wonderful, and best in the United States, but the inner life is just being discovered in America.

Is there an inner life?

Yes, there is an inner life.

But if you are foolish enough to go around and listen to people talk that is not going to do you any good. You have to wake up the inner light yourself and you live it.

I'm simply giving tools, I'm walking through life giving tools for you to wake up your inner light.

[*From a talk Paul Reps gave in June 1979*]

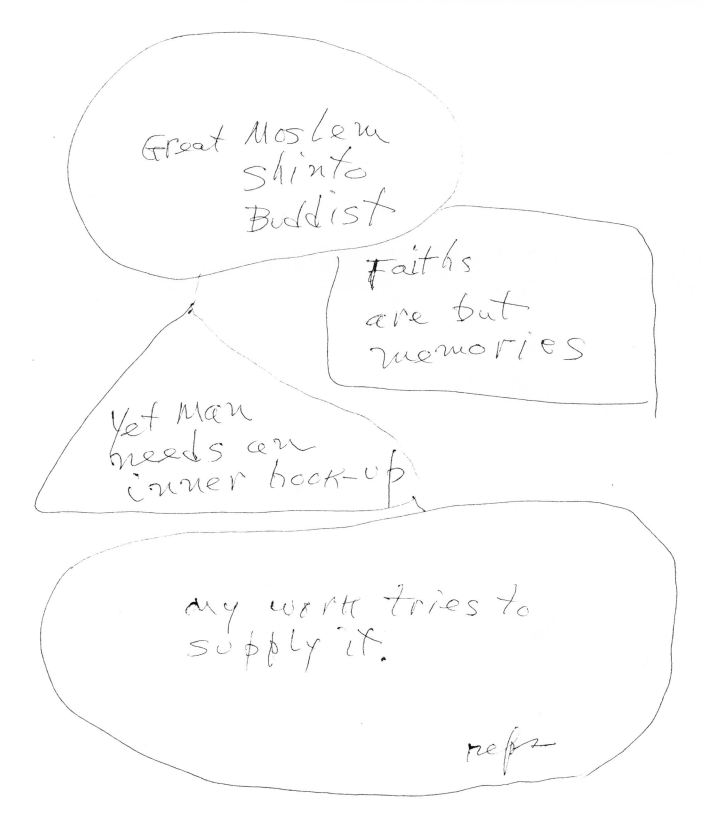

Dear Bill,

There is a wisdom greater than yours or mine. It is yours and mine as we sleep and wake and do; whereof a single cell multiplies and becomes our heart, hand, foot, our growing and our moving, us.

In this wisdom we are immersed—in wonder.

Some call it love, some God, some life. Some ignore, deny or foul it, but not for long. It is felt in anything we do or see or say, and all through nature. We cannot name it, we cannot miss it.

"Hello"
"GOODbye"
——DRAGONfly

22 Feb 55 *Cora Toon!*

Without joy, living looses its worth.
The greatest joy comes with the deepest faith.
And comes your letter so full of this faith, so strong
in signature, so essentially joyous, that I am ashamed
and thankful together.

It is I who would learn from you, and am very thankful
you took me into your home and let me taste it!

I am unable to appraise what goes on in a basketball star.
My farthest ski jump was only 72 feet, and in judo only a
brown belt.

Nor can I compute Elizabeth, namesake of my saint in France,
but something very fine is swirling around her that may
leaven the burned out soil of India in others.

Bill, and a fatigue I felt in him, are really in me,
for the man I know I know as stimuli into my awareness.
So this is my fatigue until I change it and the problem of
doing so, or of assimilating any stimulus, is my
joyous puzzle.

You say, dear Cora, "Before you know it, I will also
recapture the joy of living that was once mine."

In which pocket will you put it then - when this joy
pours off your hands continually.   Only it flows more from
reps when he is closer to the ravishing symphony of nature,
when he eats less, and when he gets out of the way.

There is a telegraph company that we can send each other
messages with. And there is another such company that has
messages travelling between each person wherever and whenever
continually.   For this communication one must be very still
and then

    someone   sends

                over the

                   ai$t$

        joy   joy

                and the

    someone

             is

          you,

Dearest Cora,

Thank you for your life.
Thank you for your housepitality
and smiling and grace. Has cat grace?

Maharshi always said
over and over
grace is everywhere.
Could it be just when you move into center?
Could it?

If it isn't everywhere can it be anywhere?

Are you?

27 Banzais from

reps   atcoreit1jgrace

BILL!
    You may be the only man in the world
    who knows how to meditate,
    the only one I have told how (partly)

And you already experienced.

There is a difference between yours and my philosophy
and the others, held in, out or what not:

        we play it

Those philosophers were specialists in puzzles,
and took themselves very seriously,
that is, they confounded themselves with words.

BUT WOMEN ARE NEVER TAKEN IN BY THEM.

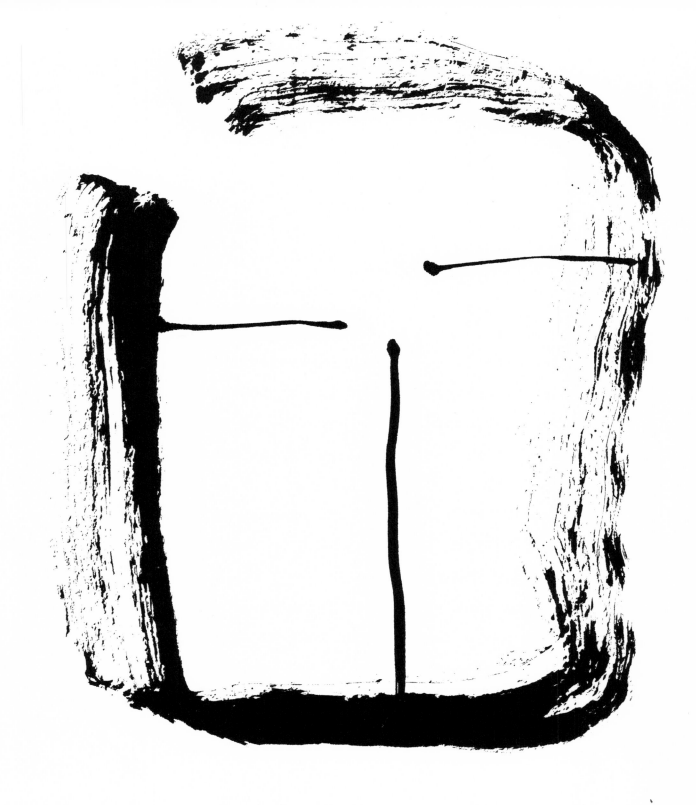

not interfering
with
me

Bill,

this is in *response* to your words saying:

> "...Always too much to do —
> how not to do
> or how to do without interrupting *be?*"

TELLGRAM

Bill, a friend sent me a booklet namod

DOGEN'S BENDOWA. It has no publisher listed but may

be an edition supplement of THE EASTERN BUDDHIST, otani

university, kyoto.   Your zendo should have a copy. Read it.

Short, to the point, dogen out-dogens himself.

THE BIG POINT IS THIS:

DOGEN PLUMPS FOR INTEGRITY experienced before concepts.

"KEEP FROM LETTING YOUR MIND HOLD TO SUPERFICIAL OR PARTIAL KNOWLEDGE."

now for your information,

this is the same as the 1st commandment.

Let me ex-plain later. When this is discovered

all faiths becoome one and we are one one-ing.

Bill,

My last letter to you solves nothing. It talks from the outside. But we discuss what we experienced, for example. This means there is a we to have experiences. Or an I.

The hypothesis is that I can see changes. If this is so, then the I is unchanging in order to be able to see them. This means in fact that *mind* does not change but senses change in *mind*.

So naturally we assume the position that
I,
mind
unchanging   observes   changes.

No doubt we meet *in* the still mind, not in the changes.

In sum,
In Tao,
Ain't it the truth?

The above gives us an entirely new view, a Tao now view.
Hui Neng and Huang Po might agree with this.

You read this in a room.
If you even think, "a room,"
that then is the unchanging background.
etc. etc.
This is what Bucky (Fuller) ought to mean by integrity,
INtegrity.

WHY NOT TRY FOR A NEW ORIENTING

If you say how, you spoil it. If you see how, you reveal it. If you are how, you are it.

it is 750,000 before

now years now

repa

Dear Bill,

Perhaps our individual Zen session experiences tune us together, both cognizant of their inadequacies. The book: THE PRACTICE OF ZEN, by Chang, gives some of the Chinese roots of Zen Japanese have formalized and stiffened.

Your once remark cooked in me ever after: "I feel we need some daily exercise." Title of my next opus: 5 chops of wood . . .

Easy to Buddha: INvigorate into balance, then turn on sound and light/delight/   But without vigor the house of cards topples: you are right.

INvigorate is to chop wood on outbreaths
thence
gradually
IN IN **IN**

Hindu presence: instant light tophead illumination

Chinese: mid eyes

American: heart

Japanese: low-down base (hence they can't explain only sit)

Dear Bill,

Say boy, if it isn't fun it's better left undone. No harm trying to formulate fun or enlightenment except that it can't be done; it just is, that's it. Zen master Soen complimenting my poems regretted he had done nothing worldshaking, but he had all the formulae which in turn weighed him down. The Chinese are free of this, being a tall big bodied people, continental and with a grassroots view that simply took over any Hinduism that leaked in. *Taoism* became *shinto* in Japan (grassroots) and *channa* became *zen*, and *Dhyana*, sanskrit, stemmed from *yoga* or one-point fixing detailed in Patanjali yoga sutras and this became *prajna*, wisdom, only it ain't.

Grand, ne ?

                                                                                reps

[*The following letter is in response to a letter from Bill saying that Roshi Suzuki and Richard Baker from the Zen Institute in San Francisco had been visiting him in New York; and that later he had also been visited by Meihoko, Dr. D. T. Suzuki's secretary.*]

big
Bill

How splendid you could meat the roshi and the stiff baker!
why was soto zen always more popular quantitatively than
rinzai? because they made it easier? is it easy?
do we need to spend $150,000. to SIT DOWN?
why not sit up?
grassblades do too.
How about Meihoko?
Instead of drugs 100 young white skinners search
a way to me with sitting. ask a potato tells how.
how to do it. dare you read it?
what are some differences between chinse and japanese
sitting? which do you prefer?
does it hurt you to sit down? where?
how about this? do you know if you sit when you sit
it gives you a big bang? really does.
you begin to laugh.
if you sit under a bridge it is better yet.
bridge is the arch between the eyes .
suzuki went back to japan and gave title to the
monastery he owned to his son so he could sit in USA
(and raise $150,000 too). Think big. Get to the
money people. What will they do with it anyway.
Take it from them. The young americans decided Roshi
shouldn't be called Reverend any more but just roshi.
it takes an american to tell a japanese how to do it.
he assented. but why was he ever called Reverend?
do you think americans can tell chinese how to do it?
what will they tell them? ask a potato. huzzah you.

Bill,

Have you tasted Suzuki sweet all thru book ZEN MIND BEGINNERS MIND wherein he dares be himself?
Very good for Zen.   See it!

Now let me give you the real low down:

Since my early days in the NYC library the mystics have most appealed to me. Of course no one understands them or anyone else.

D. T. Suzuki, my doll, the man I have been *FOR* for years, discovered them mystics and read them and said to himself, "Look here, we zanners got something even better," and so he began to zan from mystic view and it caught on because no other Japanese was unselfish enuf to tell anyone anything, so couldn't.

Really.

Light turns on light (to travel) comma-like and when anyone sits still or stops outing he begins to feel good.

So of course when he began to mysticize the zan this felt good and gooder and no doubt.

His *USE OF LIGHT* revivifies him and reflects in his use of breath, for longevity.

Suzuki my hero made a religion single handed with his eyebrows but his zen aint like the Japanese and all set in *PAST* tense.

Many thanks for R.H. Blyth book just arrived   I like it, just like I like people. Most Americans however if made to read it would utter your famous cry

HELP!

because it sets up a framework for them to crawl around in, like a Bucky dome.

Why not step outside!

Dear Bill,

Now we are continually nourished each breath from the infinite well that spews forth things, words, ideas, and all our waking goings on.

To call this well (Allah of the Muslim) (and God of the Christian) emptiness simply reverses all man's faith, in facts attacks it. We cannot attack man's faith and succeed. We have to affirm it. Buddha really never attacked man's faith but gave it a greater love.

Let me quote you from my new book in the making:

INSTANT CHAN

The Chinese are wise sitters, sitting when they do comfortably instead of formally.

They have thousands of books on ways of sitting and even a hundred will convince anyone that it can't be had in books.

One way:

Later explorers of Tao held that our life radiance stems from our core, a place located in the abdomen about three inches below the navel. Attention from here to the sex center, to the anal, then up the backbone to tophead, around and down begins the circulation of light.

Emperor Hwang-Ti, 2500 BC: "The blood current flows continuously in a circle and never stops."

Thus you observe that old emperor is still alive in you.

And I have just written an article explaining in function, how, the Taoist faith, or meditation. A Chinese who read it wrote me, "You are a wonderful man as you a american who can understand the east so deeply. You make me very surprised."

These guys have lost their own tao but it is dormant in their cells and they *know* it there, everyone of them does. I ask me why I always feel like leaving Japan and the answer comes, I get tired of their closed mind attitude/ anyway the vibrant sharp fast chinese are a good antidote/ am convinced they are all poets too but another kind; that is, they respond to anything with joy, immediacy, feeling, and a lot of apperception, as if they were dancing to some unheard music. Come at once.

A Sufi from Bhagdad gives a dinner in New York USA.
He tells the Americans they are in a bad way
because they never leave their minds.

A Zen man from Japan recommends *zazen*, still sitting.

Both mean that Americans fail to experience (gravity).

"But", a woman protests,
"my holy master floats from his seat in meditation."

The Zen man adds, "Our *zazen* is more than gravity."

Concepting, one says he is Sufi.
Concepting, one thinks himself Zen.
Concepting, using words, you read this.

But you do more than concept as you experience wholly.
Release into gravity gives a sense of levitating.
Even stones float and fly.
This work in-vites *experiencing wholly*.

"How can it when it uses words?"
It can as you let it.

A Healthy man!

ABBOT TO-LUN
GURU OF BUDDHISM

1897 SUTTER ST.
SAN FRANCISCO, CALIFORNIA, U.S.A.
10 JOY AVENUE, BRISBANE CITY
SAN MATEO COUNTY, CALIFORNIA, U.S.A.
NO. 31 WONGNEICHONG ROAD, 12 FLOOR
HONG KONG

BILL— VISIT this MAN!
He speaks little English
but he BEAMS. In a Negro
& Japanese section, he
teaches chinese meditation
meetings 1 P.M. Sunday.
You will love him.
reps, guru of fisher

BILL

To-Lun calls it
To go into abstraction

Reps says it is rhythm accord
of nervestream
In here everything gets right   Nerve pulse
                                  heartpulse
but   breathpulse
Just as you get out of sleep
what you order into it – the order
COOKS—
So similarly, if your intent
is some great good for another
and you take this into your
"time of 15" beforehand, not during
it has a best chance to come true
Here is the secret of To-Lun
miracles (his good intent
carried into the .15)
Now, Bill, you can do this too
this describes MAN-will-reflecting-
in-bliss comes about with intent.
Here, the true consecration!
FOCUS

reps

Dear Bill,

You can be against or you can be for.
You can be separative and exclusive or inclusive and loving.

Any organization like a religion that excludes
goes against the togethering trend of our times.

To include means not only to study one's own faith,
but the comparable faiths of others to find a common ground.
When nations dare no longer fight why should religions exclude?

It is the duty of anyone connected with any faith to explain it
to outsiders and this the faithful cannot do,
being ignorant of the faiths of others.

This is why religions are dying and zen and yoga are lost.

A 4000 Year Old Manuscript

Wandering in the ineffable beauty of Kashmir, I came upon the hermitage of Lakshmanjoo. It overlooks green rice fields, the gardens of Shalimar and Nishat Bagh, lakes edged with lotus and a stream of icy water rushing from a mountain top.

Here the hermit of Lakshmanjoo translated to me, in English peculiar to him, an ancient manuscript which has been recopied many times and passed through many hands throughout the centuries.

In this manuscript, 112 ways are formulated to "open the invisible door of consciousness." These ways were set forth some 4000 years ago, and are in the form of a dialogue between Shiva and Devi. Some of these directions may appear redundant, yet each is different; some may appear simple yet any one demands constant dedication.

Just as *centering* or balance is the secret of ordinary skills, so may it be the basis for the development of our greater awareness. As an experiment, try standing equally on both feet, imagine balance slightly more on one foot, then on the other. Just as balance centers, you are in the *centering* of consciousness.

If we are conscious in part, this implies more inclusive consciousness. Have you a hand? Yes. That you know without doubt, but until you were asked this question, were you aware of the hand itself?

Surely, the prophets and saints, known and unknown to the world, have shared a common *uncommon* discovery. The Tao of Lao-Tse, Nirvana of Buddha, the Father of Jesus, the God of Moses, the Allah of Mohammed, the Lover of Sufis point to the experience.

How can one transcribe an immanent teaching? It is possible less from knowledge gained from books and practice, more from being receptively free. —REPS

DEVI SAYS:

O Shiva, what is your reality? What is this wonder-filled universe? What is seed? Who centers the universal wheel? What is this life pervading forms beyond form? How can realization standing above space and time, above names and descriptions, be actualized in fullness? Let my doubts be cleared.

SHIVA REPLIES:

(Now begin the 112 instructions which are given to humanity through Devi)

1   Radiant one, this experience may dawn between two breaths. After breath comes in (down) and just before turning up (out), *the beneficence*.

2   As breath turns from down to up, and again as breath curves from up to down — through both these turns, *realize*.

3   Or, wherever inbreath and outbreath fuse, at this instant touch the energyless energy-filled center.

4   Or, when breath is all out (up) and stopped of itself, or all in (down) and stopped, in such universal pause one's small self vanishes. That is difficult only for the impure.

5   Consider your essence as light rays rising from center to center up the vertebrae, and so rises *livingness* in you.

6   Or in the spaces between, feel this *as lightning*.

7   Devi, imagine the Sanskrit letters in these honey-filled foci of awareness, first as letters, then more subtly as sounds, then as most subtle feeling. Then leaving them aside, be *free*.

8   Attention between eyebrows, let mind be before thought. Let form fill with breath-essence to the top of the head, and there shower as light.

9   Or, imagine the five colored circles of the peacock tail to be your five senses in illimitable space. Now let their beauty melt within. Similarly, at any point in space or on a wall — until the point dissolves. Then your wishes for others come true.

10   Eyes closed, see your inner being in detail. Thus come to your true nature.

11   Place your whole attention in the nerve, delicate as the lotus thread, in the center of your spinal column. In such be transformed.

12   Closing the seven openings of the head, a space between your eyes becomes all-inclusive.

13   Touching eyeballs, lightness between them opens into heart and there permeates the universe.

14   Bathe in the center of sound, as in the continuous sound of a waterfall. Or by putting fingers in ears, hear the sound of sounds.

15   Intone a sound, as A U M, slowly. As sound enters soundfulness, so *do you*.

16   In the beginning and gradual refinement of the sound of any letter, *awake*.

17   While listening to stringed instruments, hear

18 their composite central sound; thus omnipresence.

18 Intone a sound audibly, then less and less audibly as feeling deepens into this silent harmony.

19 Imagine spirit simultaneously within and around you until the entire universe is spiritualized.

20 Kind Devi, enter etheric presence pervading far above and below your form.

21 Put mindstuff in such inexpressible fineness above, below, and *in your heart.*

22 Consider any area of your present form as limitlessly spacious.

23 Feel your substance, bones, flesh, blood, lymph, saturated with cosmic essence.

24 Suppose your passive form to be an empty room with walls of skin, empty.

25 Blessed one, as senses are absorbed in heart reach the center of the lotus.

26 Unminding mind, keep in the middle *until.*

27 When in worldly activities, keep attentive between the two breaths, and so practicing, in a few days be born anew. *(Lakshmanjoo says this is his favorite.)*

28 Focus on fire rising through your form from the toes up until the body burns to ashes *but not you.*

29 Meditate on the make-believe world as burning to ashes, and become *being* above human.

30 Feel the fine qualities of creativity permeating your breasts and assuming delicate configurations.

31 With intangible breath in center of forehead, as this reaches heart at the moment of sleep, have direction over dreams *and over death itself.*

32 As subjectively letters flow into words and words into sentences, and, as objectively circles flow into worlds and worlds into principles, find at last these converge *in our being.*

33 Gracious one, play the universe is an empty shell wherein your mind frolics infinitely.

34 Look upon a bowl without seeing the sides or the material. In a few moments become aware.

35 Abide in some place endlessly spacious, clear of trees, of hills, of habitations. Thence comes the end of mind pressures.

36 Sweet-hearted one, meditate on knowing and not knowing, existing and not existing. Then leave both aside that you may be.

37 Look lovingly on some object. Do not go on to another object. Here in the middle of this object, *the blessing.*

38 Feel cosmos as translucent everliving presence.

39 With utmost devotion, center on the two junctions of breath and know *the knower.*

40 Consider the plenum to be your body of bliss.

41 While being caressed, sweet princess, enter the caressing as everlasting life.

42 Stop the doors of senses when feeling the creeping of an ant. *Then.*

43 At the start of sexual union, keep attentive on the fire in the beginning, and so continuing, avoid the embers in the end.

44 When in such embrace your senses are shaken as leaves, enter this shaking.

45 Even remembering union, without the embrace, *the transformation.*

46 On joyously seeing a long absent friend, permeate this joy.

47 When eating or drinking, become the taste of the food or drink, and be filled.

48 Lotus-eyed one, when singing, seeing, tasting, be aware you are and discover *the everliving.*

49 Wherever satisfaction is found, in whatever act, actualize this.

50 At the point of sleep when sleep has not yet come and external wakefulness vanishes, at this point *being* is revealed. *(Lakshmanjoo says this is another of his favorites.)*

51 In summer when you see the entire sky endlessly clear, encompass such clarity.

52 Lie down as dead. Enraged in wrath, stay so. Or stare without moving an eyelash. Or suck something and become the sucking.

53 Without support for feet or hands, sit only on buttocks. Suddenly *the centering.*

54 In an easy position, gradually pervade an area between the armpits *into great peace.*

55 SEE AS IF FOR THE FIRST TIME A BEAUTEOUS PERSON OR AN ORDINARY OBJECT.

56 With mouth slightly open, keep mind in the middle of tongue. Or, as breath comes silently in, feel the sound HH.

57 When on a bed or a seat, let yourself become weightless, beyond mind.

58 In a moving vehicle, by rhythmically swaying, experience. Or in a still vehicle, by letting yourself swing in slowing invisible circles.

59 Simple by looking into the blue sky beyond clouds, *the serenity.*

60 Shakti, see all space as if already absorbed in your own head *in the brilliance.*

61 Waking, sleeping, dreaming, know you as light.

62 In rain during a black night, enter that blackness as the form of forms.

63 When a moonless raining night is not present, close eyes and find blackness before you. Opening eyes, see blackness. So faults disappear forever.

64 JUST AS YOU HAVE THE SENSATION TO DO SOMETHING, STOP.

65 Center on the word AUM without any A or M.

66 Silently intone a word ending in AH. Then in the HH effortlessly, *the spontaneity.*

(please turn)

Green
so green the hills
I cannot remember
your name

67 Feel yourself as pervading all directions, far, near.

68 Pierce some part of your nectar-filled form with a pin, and gently enter *the piercing.*

69 Feel: My thought, I-ness, internal organs.

70 Illusions deceive, colors circumscribe. Even divisibles are indivisible.

71 When some desire comes, consider it. Then suddenly quit it.

72 Before desire and before knowing, how can I say I am? Consider; dissolve in *the beauty.*

73 With your entire consciousness in the very start of desire, of knowing, *know.*

74 O Shakti, each particular perception is limited, disappearing in omnipotence.

75 In truth forms are inseparate. Inseparate are omnipresent being and your own form. Realize each is made of this consciousness.

76 In moods of extreme desire be undisturbed.

77 This so-called universe appears as a juggling, a picture show. Look upon it this way to be happy.

78 DEVI, PUT ATTENTION ON NEITHER PLEASURE NOR PAIN BUT BETWEEN THESE.

79 Toss attachment for body aside, realizing *I am everywhere.* One who is everywhere is happy.

80 Objects and desires exist in me and in others. So accepting, let them be translated.

81 The appreciation of objects and subjects is the same for an enlightened as for an unenlightened person. The former has one greatness: he remains in the subjective mood, not lost in things.

82 Feel the consciousness of each person as your own consciousness. So leaving aside concern for self, become each being.

83 Thinking no thing will limited self unlimit.

84 Believe *omniscient, omnipotent, pervading.*

85 As waves come with water and flames with fire, so the universal waves with us.

86 Roam about until exhausted and then, dropping to the ground, in this dropping *be whole.*

87 Suppose you are gradually being deprived of strength or knowledge. At the instant of deprivation, transcend.

88 Listen while the ultimate mystical teaching is imparted: EYES STILL, WITHOUT WINKING, AT ONCE BECOME ABSOLUTELY FREE.

With a thousand
green wings
fig tree
flies up the alley

89 Stopping ears by pressing and rectum by contracting, enter the sound of sound.

90 At the edge of a deep well, look steadily into its depths until — the wondrousness.

91 Wherever your mind is wandering, internally or externally, at this very place, *this.*

92 WHEN VIVIDLY AWARE THROUGH SOME PARTICULAR SENSE, KEEP IN THE AWARENESS.

93 At the start of sneezing, during fright, in anxiety, above a chasm, flying in battle, in extreme curiosity, at the beginning of hunger, at the end of hunger, be uninterruptedly aware.

94 Let attention, be at a place where you are seeing some past happening, and even your form, having lost its present characteristics, is transformed.

95 Look upon some object, then slowly withdraw your sight from it, then slowly withdraw your thought from it. *Then.*

96 Devotion itself frees.

97 Feel an object before you. Feel the absence of all other objects but this one. Then leaving aside the object-feeling and the absence-feeling, *realize.*

98 The purity of other teachings is as impurity to us. In reality nothing is pure or impure.

99 This consciousness exists as each being and nothing else exists.

100 BE THE UNSAME SAME TO FRIEND AS TO STRANGER, IN HONOR AND DISHONOR.

101 When a mood against someone or for someone arises, do not place it on the person in question, but remain *centered.*

102 Suppose you contemplate something beyond perception, beyond grasping, beyond not being, *you.*

103 Enter space, supportless, eternal, still.

104 WHEREVER YOUR ATTENTION ALIGHTS, AT THIS VERY POINT EXPERIENCE.

105 Enter the sound of your name and through this sound, all sounds.

106 I am existing. This is mine. This is this. Even in such, know illimitably.

107 This consciousness is the spirit of guidance of each one. Be this one.

108 Here is a sphere of change, change, change. Through change, consume change.

109 As a hen mothers her chicks, mother particular knowings, particular doings, in reality.

110 Since in truth bondage and freedom are relative, these words are only for those terrified with the universe. This universe is a reflection of all minds. As you see many suns in water from one sun, so see bondage and liberation.

111 Each thing is perceived through knowing. The self shines in space through knowing. Perceive one being as knower and known.

112 Beloved, at this moment let mind, knowing, breath, form, *be included.*

So closes this version of a 4000-year-old love story.

As a bird tied to a string flies first in every direction and finding no rest anywhere settles down at last on the very place it is fastened, our mind after flying in every direction settles into breath.

For mind is fastened in breath.

CHANDOGYA UPANISHAD

BACK   BREATHING

[From BE!]

1

Some of us find we are breathing against ourselves some 14,000 breaths daily. This may be life-shortening.

Woodchoppers, singers, those who work rhythmically *exert with outbreath and release with inbreath*.

If we reverse this and try to exert with inbreaths, we only exert against ourselves.

Planting violence in you, I harvest it in me.

Why not plant love?

Please do.

2

Take a bath, rubbing skin vigorously. Put on a loose robe and sit comfortably still.

As mind jumps to this and that   let it while you keep IN natural breath rhythm.

This comes close to the breath of deep sleep. If you find it too easy to do, then keep attention in the *silent sound* of breath, supposing this silent sound.

If you cannot believe what you suppose, you may never play with children or sit under a tree. If you cannot suppose this *silent sound* then imagine an almost silent sound as *whoo* on outbreathflow and *whoo* on inbreathflow through nostrils.

If mind starts to twitch or itch   let it but keep IN your natural breathflow.

One of the methods of mind guidance in the Orient has been the use of *mantra* or soft sound or word. Any sound will do. It works because breath itself has a range of sound from dissonance to still harmony. Fingers in ears, we hear our disturbing become undisturbing sound. Ultimately this sound experience is to be discovered by yourself rather than imposed by another.

Suppose   a subject

Suppose an object

Suppose   no object

Suppose no subject

Surely this enoughs to set you free of
m   e

may I have
a drink of water
from the cup
of your hand

nepa

[Reps clearly enjoyed poking fun at the organizations, practices, rules and regulations of many of the Oriental teachers as they arrived to introduce their teachings in the West. It should be remembered that Reps was often a good friend of these spiritual masters, having met many of them during his travels in the East. American friends often sought out Reps' advice concerning which of these teachers he thought would be useful to study with. The letter below is a reply to a friend asking if she should study "transcendental meditation" with Maharishi Mahesh Yogi. A copy was enclosed in one of the letters to Bill.]

dear gal,

you ask if you should follow your man and take up the meditation of mahesh yogi

why ask me?
why not ask your me?

in india whenever you turn around you meet a guru

for centuries they have given mantra to do as japanese audible or silent repetition of the mantra

and this positivizes the organism that was overnegative

to charge for this priceless practice is unthinkable in India

in selling this at a high price without explaining its hindu use may be necessary
to catch ignorant foreigners and get them off drugs and get them working on the inner life

but to withold its international or organic reason for doing seems provincial

in india a person usually accepts such a treasure with love
but may if unworkable for him seek another guru
so what we put into it equates what we get out of it

ram das and his consort krishnabai
deceased now   living, the finest most INlightened
                     woman in the world
                         I had already ordered her book sent
                         you from india takes 3 months to arrive
they give the mantra openly and freely, not secretly and hokuspokusly

why not visit krishnabai!!!!!

if mahesh also wrote asking my advice if he should take an initiation from you I should say
YES you are more IT than he

in fact I have proposed a school (starting I think) in SF where all teachers
can come over world and share instead of exploit their faiths
but mahesh is better far than drugs
however transcendental means out of body, a hindu trait,
whereas cold climate folk like INbody orientations

the mahesh group meet to fortify themselves

sivananda ashram yoga camp 8th ave val morin, PQ montreal canada
and another camp in winter in bahamas sounds good
their yoga book is excellent
and they say pay what you wish

I like reps 11 WAYS TO MEDITATE to be published soon we hope

reps thinks world is coming together so everyone should share their finding
not use them for separative purposes

but in beginning separation may be needed
lots of ideas come to folks who eat sprouts

reps

Bill,

There comes a guru on every street corner
as reps ordered.

This is a new kind of culture for americans.

But something deeper is happening.
The study of Yoga is increasing enormously
because people are getting a good taste out of it.

How come?
Self discipline, no less.

The same for just sitting like stones in zen
despite the accoutrements.

Now if you could set up an advisory center
where the outsiders, the more people, could learn
about the possible benefits from these doings,
they would gladly pay for it.

This is an entirely new idea.
You join the club or take the magazine to learn
how to get in, to read what benefits others
got from it, etc.

Maybe you have 100 guru projects, with
testimonials and experiences for each, each good.
This could be a big advertisement for the sellers.

It could be an educational project survey.
If someone thinks this thru as they will
they will come up with a big success,
more than just selling a magazine to readers.

Maybe like a consumers research report
on the various teachings, saying what one
was given, how, etc. etc. and rated.

This would end up with thousands trooping around
to chinese, japanese, hindu, tibetan and other
gurus to sample and taste their wares, a huge show.

Swallow

[*In the late Sixties and early Seventies, before the advent of a wide range of "alternative" magazines and worldwide symposiums of spiritual leaders, Reps and Bill, who had "sampled the wares" of many gurus over the years, corresponded about the possibility of a magazine which would gather and make available to many, information about all the different possibilities for an inner practice. Below is a second letter from Reps about this, and there are more in Chapter 4.*]

BILL,

WE ACT FROM FEEL

You give me no reason for acting unreasonably in your new mag project *because you are acting from feel*.

FEEL also is moar feminine, that is, women are the experts in it. Also what % buy your new "x" mag? Probably women 5 to 1. And women are blank, largely blank when it comes to occult, spooky, zen sit and all the rest. They simply do not understand man's aberration. Nor do they, politics.

Actually, man is mad.

I am trying to cure you of *your* madness in short order. Too big a task? Must you go to all the trouble of making a mag to get someone to understand what *you* stand for and represent??? This is the negative side of it. The positive is **HAVE FUN** even if you ruin yourself doing it. Or, *plan* it better, better than you have so far, and *sell* the idea to a big firm like IBM and let them frankly back it!!! This is one grand idea.

maybe it is **THE** answer
we are searching for

i.e. Ford backs a Mustang for outer life and "x" for inner life. You might get 5 companies or 10 to back 5 issues. This issue backed by General Foods. A good editor with a scissors could clip all material and shorten and comment as Readers Digest does.

The best of the Gurus:

Today Guru Gitananda renounces
his guru-ship, cuts off his beard
and becomes real human-like
Refuses to play the guru game

We are going to become international with gurus and your mag is first sign of it, but it is a few years too soon. You need a man in each country to report and a head man to show how all this guff meets as one, **HE, SHE**

she is same as he
except with a *sshh* before it

a woman will do anything if
she can do it secretly

A

B

C coming world success
very hopeful for world

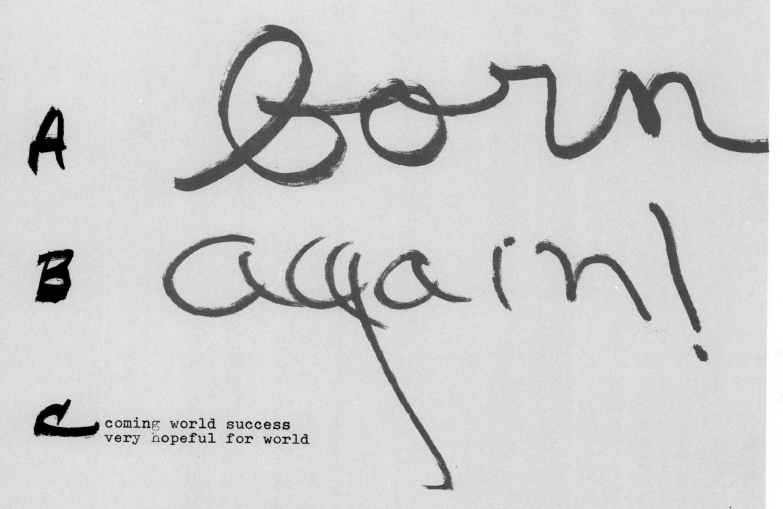

BILL

I took them at their word and have been

BORN AGAIN!

It is the religious ceremony for that
purpose by the phllipines and by the old
astecs and toltecs and mayans

if interested I will meet you in chicago
and tell you all about it when I give the
private talk there about Nov 17. If so
will let you know. The detail of it, real
or faked etc etc is INCIDENTAL to the
EXPERIENCE
you should have it   what are you living for?
PPS each AF issue shows someone has been born
again it is so bright right

Dearest Cora,

Thank you for your life.
You say ~~you~~ this: "The furthest I've
got towards solving THE PROBLEM is to
give up (which, by the way, I think
is pretty far)."

Perhaps you are a post-primitive
and Bill a primitive and reps a
pre-primitive. Now how would THE PROBLEM
look to each of these, also including the
ostriches and worm and squirm?

For me you have evaporated
erased and shortcircuited all my cares
away

reps

repstrokes

[*On brushstroking, poeming, talking and exhibiting in galleries, at colleges, in Zen monasteries and on magazine covers from Japan to Sweden*]

art is organized
and
art is expensive
and
the name art is separative

i'm just having a good time

From one grain ten thousand grains
perfect packaging
one cell buds a being
accordingly
water drips
moss glows
crane flies over
fish swims in
no one apart except in madness
laugh
cry

reps

wildricely

[From an interview with Reps in Boulder, Colorado 6/22/79]

Interviewer: When you were in Japan, is that where you learned about the calligraphy that is exhibited in your picture poems?

Reps: Yes, the Japanese are great artists with the ink brush. They use a brush like this and they draw on paper. And the water flows through the brush and the feeling flows through the water and it makes interesting variable pictures.

And so I decided: I think I can do that too. And Soen Roshi who was my friend was always taking me around to meet people and he said: "I think your best present you could give them would be one of your ink brush drawings."

So I made some casual ink brush drawings and gave them as presents because you don't go visit people in Japan without bringing some present. It's the custom there. And so I gave away careless ink brush drawings as presents. But they were mine. I had no teaching in ink brush calligraphy. And nobody needs it. All they need is a brush and some ink and to start to draw on paper and their whole subconscious begins to draw out of them. So from that start, anybody can start and have fun drawing their life up, not only ink brush, but drawing their life expression in whatever they're doing.

Interviewer: Where did you get the idea to put words together with these pictures?

Reps: Well, I thought some form of words might be acceptable so I stuck words around. Or I would make these pictures and then try to say: What in the world is that? . . .

Interviewer: . . .So when you were in Japan, you picked up calligraphy, and eventually you made picture poems. Can you show us an example of your picture poems?

Reps: . . .THE WHOLE UNIVERSE IS POURING THROUGH YOU AND OUT OF YOU AND INTO YOU AND YOU ARE ABSOLUTELY FREE.

That's my trademark. I just invented that one. That's my best picture of all.

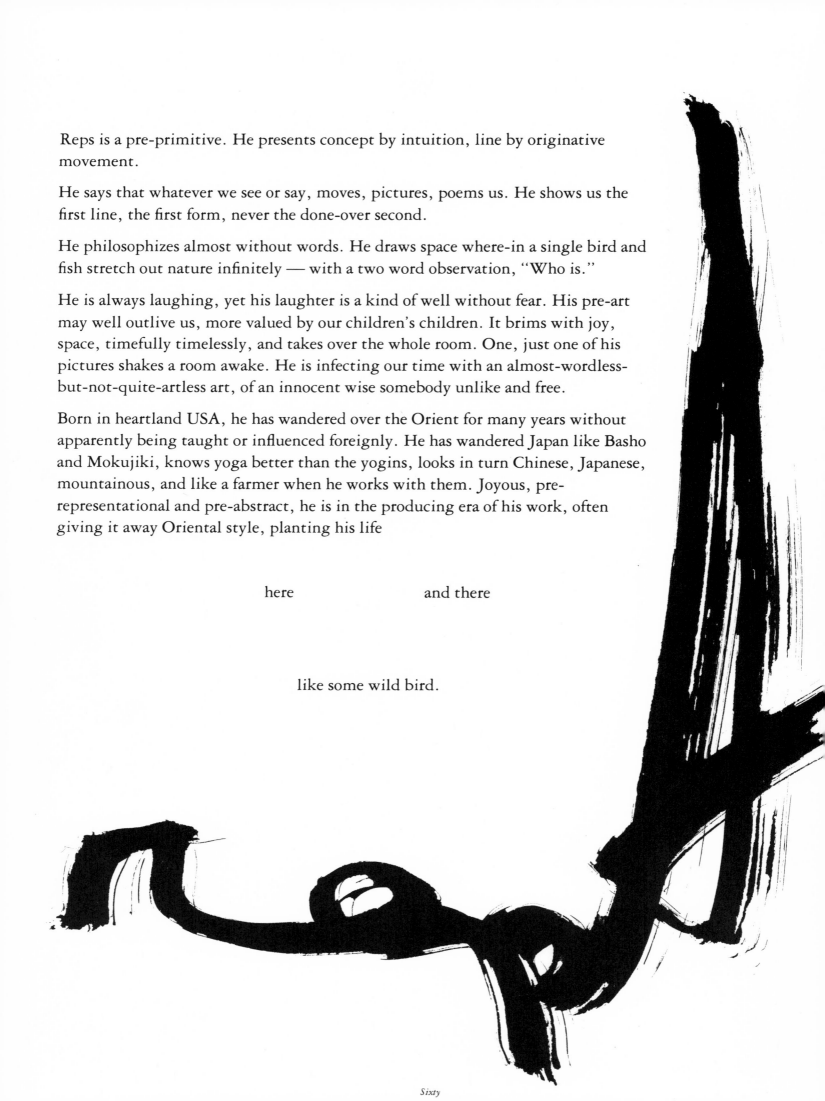

Reps is a pre-primitive. He presents concept by intuition, line by originative movement.

He says that whatever we see or say, moves, pictures, poems us. He shows us the first line, the first form, never the done-over second.

He philosophizes almost without words. He draws space where-in a single bird and fish stretch out nature infinitely — with a two word observation, "Who is."

He is always laughing, yet his laughter is a kind of well without fear. His pre-art may well outlive us, more valued by our children's children. It brims with joy, space, timefully timelessly, and takes over the whole room. One, just one of his pictures shakes a room awake. He is infecting our time with an almost-wordless-but-not-quite-artless art, of an innocent wise somebody unlike and free.

Born in heartland USA, he has wandered over the Orient for many years without apparently being taught or influenced foreignly. He has wandered Japan like Basho and Mokujiki, knows yoga better than the yogins, looks in turn Chinese, Japanese, mountainous, and like a farmer when he works with them. Joyous, pre-representational and pre-abstract, he is in the producing era of his work, often giving it away Oriental style, planting his life

here   and there

like some wild bird.

My ink-brushed lines
are so poor they are not even ugly.
They are moved from heart,
arms and hands following
care-lessly —
without training,
without thinking,
without pretending or worrying.

They are un-art, pre-art,
pre-me,
worthless
but joyously.
I don't even throw them away.

Everyone, you are making such lines
when you brush by me on the street,
when you move, writing in air
Everyone is everyone's exemplar.
We are in this together.

How poor we are, stamped on
our buttocks in sun letters,
"200 year free lease. Must be returned."
We are allowed   to write,
to move,   to brush.

The present has gone past.

                    reps

ONE
MAY BE ENOUGH
TO FREE
A ME.

BILL

    AN ARTIST IS SOMEONE DARING TO BE
HIMSELF HERSELF   FEW DO
SO FEW THAT WHEN SOMEONE DRAWS A SHE
FACING TWO WAYS OR A COW IN THE SKY
THEY THINK HE IS GREAT

    SO YOU ARE GREAT TOO

    I GIVE WORKSHOPS IN CALLIGRAPHY
TEACHING THAT A FREE LINE IS BETTER THAN
YEARS OF BRUSH TRAINING
 ALSO I GIVE DIPLOMA

BE YOU

HOWEVER TO PURIFY YOU EAT LESS OR
CHANGE EATING HOURS, CERISH YOUR
INSPIRATION AND TAKE A WARM WATDR SHORT
ENEMA EACH MORNING

NO ONE EVER IS BORN OR DIES BUT THEY
THINK THEY DO
        HOW ABSURD CAN WE GET!

each moment an unforseen mastery

[Reps has been giving "Calligraphy Class" in his books and in talks for many years. Here is one of his best classes, from his book SQUARE SUN SQUARE MOON.]

WRITING WITH WATER

CALLIGRAPHY AS THERAPY

Give a child a crayon and it will start to draw on wall or paper. Behold, a line!

The line comes before meaning. Each mark is fresh. No life movement is repeated. This is why calligraphy is therapy and calligraphers live long lives in the Orient. The vibration through their writings has been found to be the same before and after they leave this earth, according to Occidental instrumental tests.

Write largely on wall or into air to feel better.

Baby sees tree, points, "Tree!" Later a language about it follows "This is a tree." But not in Chinese or Japanese.

Their language made of picture-words shows

Tree.

Blossom.

Dog.

Run.

They often draw such pictures, finger on palm, to explain what they mean, a kind of picture thinking. They sentence themselves less.

Almost everyone has seen Chinese calligraphy, characters originally picture-drawings written with a brush dipped in rubbed black ink. In China and in Japan they are considered a primary form of art. Simply by looking into them, one perceives the person of the one who drew them much as a hand-writing expert does from ordinary script.

Picture then 25 or 30 boys and girls from 4 to 25 years of age seated on tatami in a small house they and their parents built together, a number of open newspapers before each one, a large ink brush and bowl of water to the right. They are members of a group in rural Japan near Himeji City in Hyogo. Many of the parents are farmers.

After sitting completely still for some time, a youth lifts the brush, dips it carefully in water, and draws a single line on the paper. The brush is then put down and the person rests. Or, an entire calligraphic character may be drawn with sweeping lines.

This is done in silence. Perhaps one of the instructors may show how a letter is made, even taking the brush-hand of the child in his or her own and helping with a first letter. After any assistance, the pupil bows silently in appreciation.

"Draw this line," they have been told previously, "only as you feel it to be the most worthwhile act of your life."

"Draw it with your breath."

"The line flows from brush with outbreath, although variations of it change as breath changes."

"Let the line come from and go on to infinity off the tip of the brush."

"It is less drawn than experienced."

"Not only brush, hand, arm, but heart and mind draw it." In Japanese, one word, *kokoro*, stands for both heart and mind.

"Your line is an everywhere point and curve."

"The line, not aiming at perfection, never ends."

"Let center draw through you."

Do this brush stroke over and over as the youth does, each time newly.

After 100 or 1,000 such strokes done with utmost consideration, a great harmony of motion sings through you. You feel more than elated. Your mind has entered the line and universe.

How may this come about simply by writing with water on newspaper by people who are too poor to buy unprinted paper and inks?

When we do something repeatedly, our nerves-muscles-ligaments learn how to do it more easily. This happens in riding a bicycle, in chopping wood, in singing a note, or whatever our tasks. The organism gets the idea and takes over. We may call it the subconscious mind. Until we educate this mind, we have only learned superficially. To live what we know, we must do so with our entire being. This being thrives in harmony of motion, in composure, in intelligent guidance.

Practice is a way. Breath is a way. Poise is a way. After these are gone beyond, we experience our true nature, more than something called this or that mind.

The drawing is not called *Shuji*, calligraphy, but *O-Shuji*, the drawing of God, if you wish to so translate deepest honor. It is a way of life.

Unruly pupils who come soon become cooperative. A teacher sits beside one in turmoil, simply sits, and then shows how to move brush with breath. Even in a few minutes the pupil composes within. No attention is given to changing an individual, yet immediate changes for the better are observed in students.

If you are inclined to rush or fume *O-Shuji* soon relieves unguided impulses. No part of arm is tensed. Should you feel it while it is moving, it would be soft and pliable. The brush is drawn over the paper, never pushed.

The shape of the character drawn does not matter. It is the one drawing who matters. Almost everywhere these days we find the drawing or product valued and the producer neglected. Things have become of more value than their makers.

In writing with water, a child's health often improves. It is said that even if you think of your favorite line while ailing, you feel better. This could be so, as tensions are relieved with visualized movements.

The writing proceeds in silence. After this weekly hour the tools are laid away, the newspapers dried. No laughing or joking occurs at this time, for managing oneself is more than play. With such practice one easily becomes an artist in everyday living.

To avoid any weariness, the character drawn is changed, yet only a single line is needed to discover *who* is doing what.

Sometimes what you draw surprises you. "Did I do this?" you may ask. "I could not do so. It must be *center*."

There is a center of you, a center everywhere in and through you. Once touched, life freshens. It may be touched in a brush stroke or in whatever we are doing.

So if we get some newspapers, brush and water, and try this, what happens?

We miss the presence of and respect for a teacher and through the teacher for ourself. We give up before 1,000 of 10,000 strokes. We lack the confidence of a group. Our breath habits tighten. We think instead of surpassing ourself.

And doing so we lose our greatest treasure — the opening of our unwritten everywhere *center*.

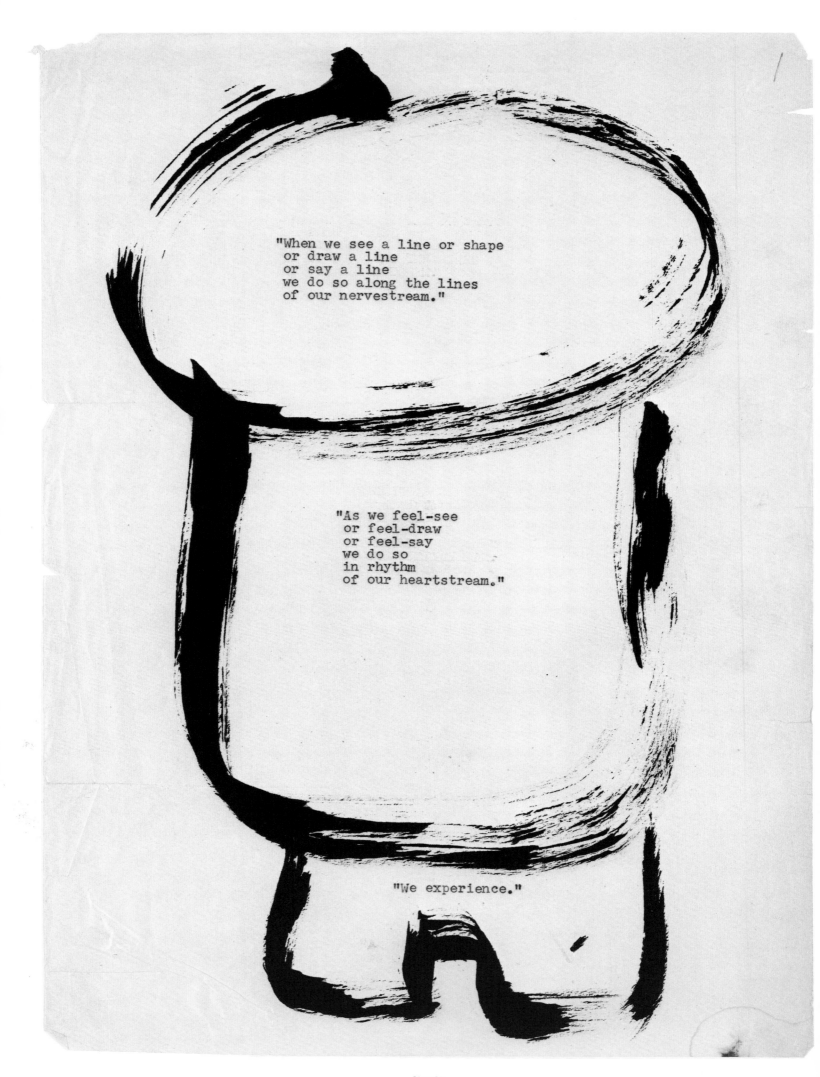

"When we see a line or shape
 or draw a line
 or say a line
 we do so along the lines
 of our nervestream."

"As we feel-see
 or feel-draw
 or feel-say
 we do so
 in rhythm
 of our heartstream."

"We experience."

These poems are nothing much to see or say
but to INsee much that fresh moves through.
Dare we be child, free of the
burden of fixed beliefs?

At a moment between sleep and waking
in our deep living consciousness
what turns to *who*.

Here play and thanks and joy
are possible.

Here in our true moment
of innocence
the ask is
granted.

Such poems would ask
for discovery
and delight
for all
of us.

reps

bud
adoring
sun

reps

The one who says I in me
and in the grassblades
is.
Our word, is, pictures an i,
a man or match stick with curving
company, s.

Let a circle picture all of me.
Let it divide into man in his true nature, I,
and his natural functions:
$$(O - - - - \frac{natural}{functions})$$

Let all between these signify
his suffering, troubling, struggling,
hating, fearing, trying, borning, dying —
a big laugh in necktie and high heels.

Why laugh at suffering?
You can as you stand as I.
How do you stand as I?
You do nothing else but.

who
is

HIEROGLYPH (picture-writing) / || |||

OF I AND YOU

reps

I pictures upright man. So he says 'I'.
The vertical tree of the cross
The active transforming stroke
The backbone
A line of light into earth -

Y ::   The erect man with arms open to sun
◊ ::   The feminine enclosing egg
U ::   The open arms, the cup to be filled -

Communication, and art, starts with vertical and
horizontal lines,
the sun line into earth
~~dayxandxnight~~   creative - receptive
male - female.

Forms are made of a multiplicity of lines.
Lines are made of light, of invisible electro-magnetic rays.
<u>So</u> <u>we</u> <u>are</u> <u>light</u>.
To <u>feel</u> and to <u>actualize</u> this, i-magine innumerable lines
of light opening up ~~our~~ <u>consciousness.</u>
Be more than half-human : be both creative and receptive
instantly, so joyous, so gentle!

If we open a book
intuitively
we are shown the page for us;
our entrance into
immediate reality.

Searching out and in this reality,
we flip to another page.
Still,
we find the image for us,
the one we actually experience.

We see a tree.
We draw in us, originatively,
the vertical line of tree.

This holds true if we draw it visually
or on white paper with black ink.

If the paper is soft
and our intent free
we draw a living line.

This experiencing
The drawing of innumerable lines
into form, belongs to everyone.

Doing it, each one is best
since it flows originatively
through each one of us.

perhaps some such "lining" prompted reps to first adventure into his easy-going amusing
picture-poems that may be yours most vividly as you yourself start to "draw" them.

brushing past

I ask forgiveness
of the branches

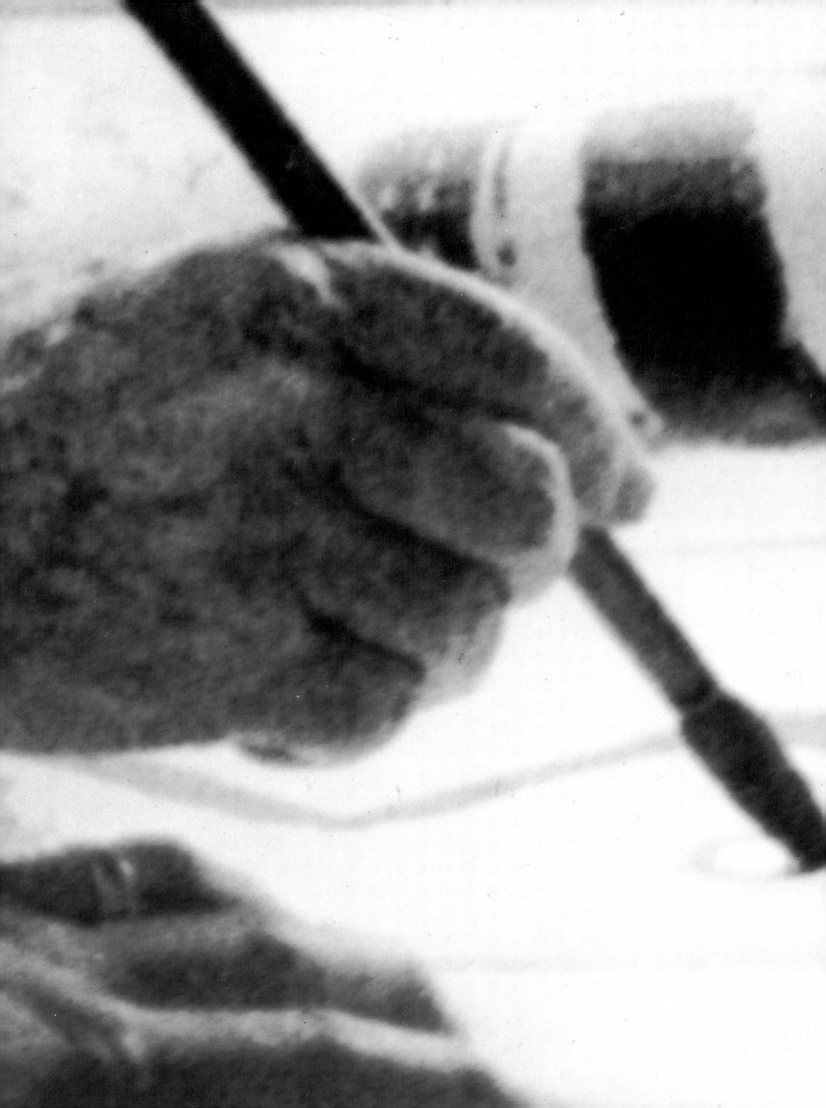

[In the late 1950's Reps brushstrokes/picture poems began to appear all over the world. As we see in the following pages, they have surfaced in his books, in shows, in talks, in homes, in Zen monasteries and even on magazine covers.

Reps is continually searching for new ways to show his art so it can be seen fresh. He has hung his picture poems from bamboo poles, letting them wave in the breeze, and he has mounted them on huge scrolls packed in fine oriental wooden boxes. Is he looking for the "best" way? "Each one is best."]

Bill,

You have played a sly trick on me, rejecting the elegant cover design I submitted to you and making one out of my simple *AH OH* poem. I hope you say inside cover *AH OH* poem by reps. One should not lift poemry.

It took me a long time to discover you are telling me poemry is better than elegance!

Admitted.

Now it's the second poem which has got noted. First *NOW NOW* / naming a newspaper published in Kyoto and also a Swedish magazine, and *AH OH* on AF face.

Thank you.

BILL

You probably know Appel's work, early work

(when the Dutch mocked at him, a Dutchman)

in cloakroom of municipal museum Amsterdam

one done 1951 on walls of Geementemuseum,Hague

like child art

so happy

so freeing so colorful

       let this be an example to us

      now his work is more arty

      now he has recognitions

      now

      it's less happy

He got money

he lost his joy

O my!

     xThis

     I suppose

     is what's dulling about art

     this outdoing oneself, trying, making
               valuable, holding onto

hope it aint me

```
dear bill,

my various picture poems are
being used in zen monasteries
as instructions.  chion-in has
a large screen of them;
various others also have them
as treasures.


lots of fun


o my,
```

MILLION-DOLLAR MONET   [*From* Newsweek, *December 25, 1967*]

The purchase of Claude Monet's painting "La Terrasse a Ste. Adresse," which New York's Metropolitan Museum recently acquired through a London dealer at Christie's auction house for a record-smashing $1,411,200, has triggered a host of staggering price comparisons. Unveiled last week amidst a superb display of fourteen of the 35 Monets the Met already owns, the picture cost more than any other modern painting, cost three times the established record auction price for a Monet ($500,000 for "On the Cliffs"), cost nearly twice the established record auction price for any other impressionist painting ($800,000 for Cezanne's "Maisons a L'Estaque").

"Besides, it is one of the first impressionist paintings ever done," says the Met's director, Thomas Hoving. "It is also one of the finest impressionist paintings ever done; it's on a par with 'The Bar at the Folies Bergeres' by Manet and 'Women in the Garden' by Monet himself." Painted and sold in 1867 for $80 when the penniless Monet was 27, the 38½ by 51-inch work is a sun, sea and wind picture in which Monet's father, seated in a cane chair, looks past a lush spring garden and some elegantly dressed friends to a boat-filled sea.

Last week The New York Times needled the Metropolitan in an editorial that coupled the recently announced fake Greek horse with the new Monet, which it called "a tasteful Monet at a tasteless price." "Tasteful!" exclaims Hoving. "It's anything but tasteful. That's like saying a girl has a nice personality. It's primitive, raw, one of the most forceful statements of nature in the history of art." And Hoving added, "A quality museum must buy quality works, and they cost."

what price a relps drawing?

BILL,

My idea of a show would be:

    one room under glass

    one room fine scrolls

    one room the chinese made scrolls

    and one room or area with six picture poems, perhaps under glass, but with prose interpretations alongside.

Anyone seeing it in a room by itself might say: "Well, that doesn't say much. I already experience any art, so why all this talk about it?"

In a remark like that the ego is nourished and the pure experience *used*. The point is very fine, but if we really appreciate *experiencing*, a good art is as well as a bad art, and all our values are undone. It is too much.

          rePS

        too much

hen we see our whole life has been an educated joke on us

[*From The Mainichi, Tokyo, 6/28/57*]

Paul Reps' Works On Display In Kyoto

— *'Pictures Before Art, Poems Before Words'* —

KYOTO.—Unique works of Paul Reps, American poet-painter, now on display at the Sankakudo Gallery, Kawaramachi Sanjo-sagaru, here, are creating a profound impression upon visitors.

The exhibition of Reps' works together with those of Kenseki Shimaoka is entitled "Pictures Before Art, Poems Before Words."

"A picture is a thing. A thing has no value. It is dead —finished. Only human beings have value," the American poet-painter said.

"My before-art blotches and before-words poems are to expose this worthlessness, to break down our human attachment to things. A picture or a poem as words only have value because the white space around them...the pause between the mere words."

He elaborated on his theory thus: "The more unoccupied space there is in a picture, the more value it will have. Japanese artists have known this for centuries, known the use of suggestion. It is the space, the no-thingness, which shows the power surging through, not an apple or a chair or a table as a thing. For this reason it must follow that a completely empty canvas must be more valuable than a filled one. It has endless potentiality. A done picture is done."

Asked why he is showing his pictures then, he replied:

"I am showing blotches or suggestive lines on clean paper ...ugliness into the perfectly pure clean universe to undo art or precede it."

Every work of his on exhibition is an illustration of his poems. He said he began to write poems as soon as he was born. Every man is a poet. When man speaks joyously, a poem is flowing out, he said.

The exhibition will last until June 30.

Legend

1. A scene of the gallery.
2. "Drinking a bowl of green tea I have stopped the war."
3. "Pine drinking luminous dew as if nothing had happened."
4. "Sometimes in May rain I can hear my fingernails growing."

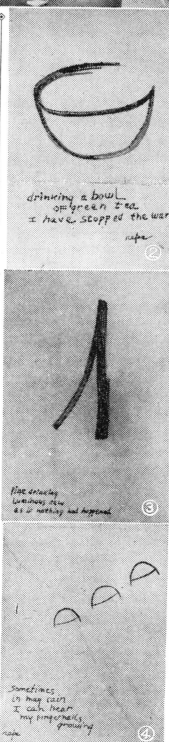

drinking a bowl
of green tea
i have stopped the war
reps

pine drinking
luminous dew
as if nothing had happened

Sometimes
in may rain
i can hear
my fingernails
growing
reps

Dear Bill,

It is my opinion the reps picture poem show may be five hundred years in advance of the designers, or at least show *ideas* rather than lovely forms. It is working in another (unseen) world. It is truly heart washings.

I also have pictures of other reps shows that could add to your ammunition in case you wish to try for a NYC show.

People walked in the San Francisco one, began to look and read and smile and enjoy — delightingly — quite different from when somberly looking at art in an art gallery show. From this experience I have the confidence to do a splendid NYC show.

All I need is some rough bamboo. 25 long stalks.

Dear Bill,

Why should fine folk ask so urgently for the unknown artless ugly reps stuff? You may answer this one.

P.S. The word *fish* is more alive than the word *nez*, spelled backwards, always will be. Instead of trying for space let us try for the space *in* fish. *Fish no like dish*. One Japanese who knew no English said this was the only poem in the exhibit he could understand.

Moral: Reps is at war with sentencing ourselves. We need imaging, sounding; the Chinese know this instinctively so well, thru their ideograms. This may bring art and US alive.

Second hand living and facing will no longer do.

GOTEBORG

Dear Bill,

I think the show in Goteborg, Sweden went big because people are eager for "Please Not Art Red Berries;" they like play, like philosophy and humor and go for low prices. (None of my new style were in it). Key to show success is to sell the whole thing out, not as art but as pre-art or picture poems, something different.

Art is too damned stiff.

This trend of course is away from scrolls; we had one big one in show (like the one I sent you) and it carried the rest. Unplanned joy, boy, lets.

Nothing to lose but our pains.

Driving into the Swedish forest village of Are, pronounced 'are-y,' I saw an interesting young man with a beard and a young woman with exotic sandals.

In the tourist bureau they came in, said a few words to the guide and left. He translated into English: "They told me they saw you in Goteborg."

Later I met them on the street. The girl had been taking tickets at the Konstmuseum, modern wing, when I picked up a Japanese on the street and pulled him in to have a look, refusing to pay her admission for a few minutes.

The man suggested I put my picture poems on newspaper and have them given away by newspapers in Sunday supplements.

Take a newspaper in your hands, front and back, without the insides. Fold it once, then again, and I found I had a 16 page book or folder, enough for any of my short books yet each page almost type letter size and big poems, 16 pages including 1 and 16 for front and back cover.

I think I will do all my books this way. No cover, no binding, no trimming - the reader invests his own interest in it by cutting some of the pages himself. What he gets is poemry.

In Japan in 1952 I gave away 30 of my scribble poems to a Japanese poet. "If you are going to be so generous I will get an exhibit for you," he said. So he collected a lot of glass for them to go under. "You can't put me under glass," I told him. I had him get a lot of bamboo we tied together as a bamboo structure on which I stuck the paper poems as washing. The wind helped everything to move. It was a great success.

One of the pictures was two small feet in black ink with the words 'now now'. These words were taken as the name for a newspaper, published many years now, *Ima Ima* , 'now now'.

In 1965 and 1966 I had exhibits of my work in Good Konst Gallery, Goteborg, with a lot of publicity from the newspapers and many enjoyed the showings. I also gave a talk last year at the Great Konstmuseum.

This year, 1967, I had a two day exhibit there. The poems were strung up on crossing lines like washing. Paper clips held them. Suddenly on the afternoon of the first day five newspaper persons came to see me with photographers. This resulted in a burst of publicity in 5 papers, the chief one a front page story with color.

It happened that the large room selected was extremely hot the night of the talk. So I said instead of an hour's talk I would give three talks of 20 minutes each with breaks. At the first break they stormed the book table and bought out all my ASK A POTATO and the ZEN FLESH ZEN BONES books. We completely forgot the heat. Gosta Ena, a young Swede, one of the six best folksingers in the country by contest, sang and played two numbers on his guitar. He had written me that my coaching was somewhat responsible for his winning, and it was his way of showing thanks.

Who wants this poor poem? I asked. Hands went up, too many, and 51 picture poems were given away as my act of devaluing art in museums.

Afterwards, curator, Nils Ryndel, said: "I told you you could never duplicate such attendance and publicity in the next year, but now I see there will be twice as many coming if you speak again." Later I suggested he have a spring festival with three poem talks and three different modern bands of and for youth and for fun, with a small charge for admission, students (of life) free. Surely festive is preferable to arty.

Some years previously I wandered into Goteborg and discovered a huge Buddha upstairs. The attendants downstairs told me they had no postcard of this piece. I told them they should have. Just then the curator came in, overheard me and invited me upstairs where he gave me a picture of this happy fellow. He also gave me a note to a stranger named Nils Ryndel, a thin, tall, smiling, adventurous, friendly Swede, with a sculptress wife and two tall children.

If I hadn't taken this chance, if I hadn't met the Chinese Buddha, my exhibits in Goteborg would never have come about and there would have been no festival.

It is probable we meet only the persons in this world we deserve to meet, or are supposed to meet, or are drawn to meet, like certain water drops down a stream gliding over certain stones on their way to the sea.

VANCOUVER

dear bill,

150 smart youth at VCR reps
workshop 9:59 AM Oct 13

they the tibetans put up such a
handsome poster for reps they
were stolen at once

so they made a cheaper one no
one would take

so to reward the takers I made
this page and gave one to each

it says *ARISE* reps.

BUT WILL HE?

Dear Bill,

My 3 talks at Dartmouth were fine. They began following me around to each one.
My 2 talks at Franconia netted $150 for wiggling my lower jaw, and the (drugged) kids went for them.
Now they want me to return to Montreal for one large audience talk and 3 smaller ones.

PAUL REPS   [*From* The University of Colorado Daily, *Boulder, 5/12/67*]

"Who is he?" I said to myself as he autographed my leg. He looks like anybody's jolly grandfather—twinkling eyes, bermuda shorts, a bright red polo shirt. But he said: "I have extracted the honey from Oriental cultures and I will deliver it to you Friday night. It is both sweet and sour. Taste for yourself."

And he said: "In my two new books, ASK A POTATO and SQUARE SUN SQUARE MOON, I express my philosophy—directly in the case of POTATO and obliquely in the other. My philosophy proposes to reorient the nervous system of man and change the world mind. However, I found the world mind was in me so I had to change myself. If this is possible, we need tools or methods to reorient and regenerate 'me' if I am over five years of age."

These tools or methods, he said, are the subject of his work. How old are you Mr. Reps? "Twenty-two. How old do you feel?"

Where do you live, Mr. Reps? "All over the world." And he said: "I have compacted the philosophies of India, Japan and China for you so you can use them immediately. My poetry is philosophy, but it is more than that. From it you can learn functional methods to guide yourself."

Mr. Reps is an authority on Zen. He has taught at Zen Center in San Francisco—"I tell them how to do it." Zen, he said, is the realization of one's true nature; it is inner living instead of outer living. It is living in instead of being thrown off, put out by situations, by people, by yourself.

Mr. Reps travels a great deal every year. Hawaii is his home. He writes and draws ("Those pictures—I'm the mother of those.") His books have been published world-wide. Among his works are ZEN FLESH, ZEN BONES,—a collection of Zen and pre-Zen writings—and ZEN TELEGRAMS, a book of picture poems.

ZEN TELEGRAMS is enchanting. In it Mr. Reps has combined simple calligraphy-inspired drawings and . . . can I say poems? No, thoughts. He calls them "weightless gifts." And they are: flashes of beauty and meaning which linger, unaccountably, so that you must turn back and look again.

Find out why he says: "Unless we can communicate simply and directly we are blocked. We must remove the blockages. We must become joyous again."

HAWAII

I, now named reps, have just heard that Goodwill President reproduced below notes and sent to each of 40 in a 3 lecture series given Feb. 1961 in Honolulu to the elite — after similar talks successful at University of Hawaii. He also stated that the $400 raised by the talks enabled them to employ two persons and start them on work that will provide them with permanent employment. These notes were not intended for distribution.

This is what you should have learned to be earned from 3 hours with reps:

He should have slowly leisurely surprisingly got it into your subconscious to lengthen your life 5 or 10 years by the infinitesimal lengthening of the outbreath. This should increase your oxygen intake and hence make for welling.

Then all sorts of good things should happen to you from this, what, who can say?

You should have picked up the idea of no worry, no hurry, no fear, ease, fun, careful consideration, just from your being, from your breathing, from your sitting or standing or moving.

In short, you should become an entirely fresh new being.

This may be possible since our cells are completely remade every 28 days.

In other words, reps was trying to get to talk with your deep being, not your surface intellectual 'knowing' writing down mind. He was sparring and breaking and suddening and spontaneousing to get into your under-mind that there is really nothing to trouble about at all.

Now, if you still want to trouble, strain and worry hurry, reps is more than happy to have you do so and to learn from you how not to do.

If even after his admonishments, you forget to chop wood—if your lifebreath is reversed—then you should see your doctor, one of the shortest-lived professions.

Of course his was only a refresher for beginning conversation. Perhaps he knows a thing or two more. Anyway he was talking with you alone, and trying to talk functionally, un-intellectually.

Next time different: Cool jazz, horizontal rest, wake, move, much more move, comforting *SIT*, walk, wine, laugh, and more jazz by Bernstein or Barati; a real session! Limited to 22 who are or feel or declare I am 22.

IS your head on straight?

What's the idea of this drawing and question?

When you let your head float up *from back*, it softens seeing, releases jaw and stretches nerves of head and backbone, so you feel good all over.

Each drawing, as easy as play tries to have you feel good all through

The letters about the drawing are celebrating too — that is, charging your cells with energy or something.

BUT PLAY IT!

in

out

Free

An original anything
is worth much more
than a duplicate.

This means you
and what you do
and how you do it.

No one ever finds
two pebbles, leaves,
persons the same,
no two times, places,
faces.

One Picasso painting
sells for 3 million dollars.
What will one reps original
bring the fortunate buyer?
Reps' books are irreplaceable
treasures while he lives.

Warning: A Korean hand reader
says he can live over 100.
He is only 85 today, September 15, 1980.

[*From a talk in Boulder, Colorado 6/12/79*]

I wrote a wonderful poem today.
There was a hole in the door, it broke,
somebody hit it and broke the plywood door.

So I took a brown piece of paper
and I pasted it over that hole and I wrote my best poem:

AS IF.   AS IF.
So   *AS IF.*

A great poem is a philosophy, it destroys everything.

Or: Do it *as if* it were so.

Or: Do it *as if* you were doing it.

I should copyright that.

AS IF.

Dear Bill,

Let me offer you for a cover
of your grand magazine my poem   *AS IF.*

It is my notion that if you use these
common uncommon words for your cover,
the following may result:

a)   You will support me $100 worth of physical survival,
b)   All human wars and worry may end by taking things more lightly, *as if.*

This reminds me of a longer reps poem occupying a full page of a Hindu magazine:

> where is Buddha?
> where is Jesus?
> *in* the dust.

> where is John?
> where is Mary?
> *in* the must.

> Holograms show us that each item is in each other item
> so Buddha and Jesus are actually *in* our dust.

> Common observation shows us
> people are *musting*
> all over the place,

> Rest assured,

reps

PS   Vashista, teacher of Rama, taught him we are completely free,
     but that we make up our dream world with percepts and concepts.

> Just be yourself.

drinking
a bowl of
green tea
I stop the war

Dear Bill,

My tourist 2-month and 2-month renewal visa for Japan having expired, I got the various complex papers together and applied for a 1-year commercial visa at the Japanese Consulate in Hongkong. "We will have to send these papers to Japan," they told me. "But that will take a month and it is costing me money to wait here for them," I said, "Please make an exception in my case." "No exceptions are possible," they told me, "not under any circumstances."

Three days later I returned with the papers and agreed to wait a month for the visa. But I included with them a poem on golden paper:

> Drinking a bowl of
> green tea
> I stop the war.

On the back of it I wrote, "A chinese says I stopped the war with this poem. If you believe such a poor *sumi-e* poem could stop the war, please give me a visa to stay in Japan for 100 years and enjoy the kind courteous people there." The man came out from the inner office. "Come back tomorrow for your visa," he said. On the morrow I returned to receive a Cultural Subjects visa good for a year's stay and good for multiple journeys for 4 years.

This is what a poem can do for a you.

reps collected

[Brushstroke poems
reproduced on fine
oriental paper and excerpts
from forty years
of Reps' books]

these writings and drawings
gathered from reps' life
free me (you)
already free

Matajuro Yagyu was the son of a famous swordsman. His father, believing that his son's work was too mediocre to anticipate mastership, disowned him.

So Matajuro went to Mount Futara and there found the famous swordsman Banzo. But Banzo confirmed the father's judgment. "You wish to learn swordsmanship under my guidance?" asked Banzo. "You cannot fulfill the requirements."

"But if I work hard, how many years will it take me to become a master?" persisted the youth.

"The rest of your life." replied Banzo.

"I cannot wait that long," explained Matajuro. "I am willing to pass through any hardship if only you will teach me. If I become your devoted servant how long might it be?"

"Oh, maybe ten years," Banzo relented.

"My father is getting old, and soon I must take care of him," continued Matajuro. "If I work far more intensively, how long would it take me?"

"Oh, maybe thirty years," said Banzo.

"Why is that?" asked Matajuro. "First you say ten and now thirty years. I will undergo any hardship to master this art in the shortest time!"

"Well," said Banzo, "in that case you will have to remain with me for seventy years. A man in such a hurry as you are to get results seldom learns quickly."

"Very well," declared the youth, understanding at last that he was being rebuked for impatience, "I agree."

Matajuro was told never to speak of fencing and never to touch a sword. He cooked for his master, washed the dishes, made his bed, cleaned the yard, cared for the garden, all without a word of swordsmanship.

Three years passed. Still Matajuro labored on. Thinking of his future, he was sad. He had not even begun to learn the art to which he had devoted his life.

But one day Banzo crept up behind him and gave him a terrific blow with a wooden sword.

The following day, when Matajuro was cooking rice, Banzo again sprang upon him unexpectedly.

After that, day and night, Matajuro had to defend himself from unexpected thrusts. Not a moment passed in any day that he did not have to think of the taste of Banzo's sword.

He learned so rapidly he brought smiles to the face of his master. Matajuro became the greatest swordsman in the land.

[*DIRECTIONS: This collection of Reps' drawings on oriental paper has been hand-folded so that you may see them one at a time or as an exhibit of eight in a row.*

TO UNFOLD THE LEFT-HAND DRAWINGS: *Lift the lower left-hand corner of "Well Silently Overflowing" and pull gently to the left until four drawings extend out of the book.* TO RE-FOLD: *Flip the entire fold-out over to the right so that the back sides of the drawings face up. Then fold the last three drawings on your right back over to the left. Now these three drawings are face up, and "Planning, Scheming . . ." is face down. Next fold the two drawings on your left over to the right so "Prison Bars . . ." covers "Bud Adoring Sun". Finally, fold "Well Silently Overflowing" back to the left.*

TO UNFOLD THE RIGHT-HAND DRAWINGS: *Turn to the last drawing, "The Rain, Yes The Rain". Lift the lower right corner and pull gently to the right until all four drawings extend out of the book.* TO RE-FOLD: *Flip the entire fold-out to the left so that the back sides of the drawings face up. Fold the last three drawings on your left back over to the right. Now these three drawings are face up while "How The Roots Must Be Laughing . . ." is face down. Now fold the two drawings on your right back over to the left so "Standing In The Rain . . ." covers "Who Is". Finally fold "The Rain, Yes The Rain" back to the right.*]

when looking into one
of these picture poems
what happens?

well
silently
overflowing

who
is

the rain
yes
the rain

[one of Paul Reps' latest works.]

IN THE LAND OF ZO

Once upon a time while strolling through the land of Zo (Oz is upside down for Zo) I came upon a *ball of light.* It seemed to be both she/he, both young/old, both out/in and all-knowing and extremely beautiful. It permeates me all over.

I ask, "Pardon me, but may I ask who you are?'

He/she replies, **THE ONLY BE-ING.**

"I never knew there was an only be-ing," I observed.

THERE WASN'T. THERE IS. SINCE PAST PRESENT FUTURE ARE NO WHERE BUT HERE AS WE MAKE THEM.

Excited, I ask, "What shall I do with my life?

After a long long long pause he/she replies, **DO NO THING AT ALL. LET DO. AS YOU TOTALLY RELEASE ALL DOING YOU COMPREHEND.**

These words seep into me like electricity. I do nothing. Perhaps we all do nothing too.

NOT ENOUGH, he/she advises. **TRY LESS HARD. JUST FOR YOU LET TRY THIS SECRET WAY. FLOAT ON YOUR BACK ON LAND OR IN WATER. DRAW TOES TOWARD KNEES AND PUSH HEELS OUT ALTERNATELY SLOWLY AS IF RIDING A BICYCLE WITHOUT LIFT-ING LEGS.**

NOW STOP. RELEASE ANY AREA STILL TIGHT.

Although stopping I feel me floating and feeling much better than best. My old self-im-posed tightnesses dissolve. "No one will know me," I think.

STOP, she/he orders. **AND DON'T MISS FUNNING.**

"Funning?" I ask.

CHILDREN SOMEHOW ALWAYS SEEM TO HAVE FUN. ARE YOU OVER FIVE? HERE YOU ARE FUNNING: UP DOWN YOUR NERVEFLOW THROUGH YOUR SPINAL COLUMN, THROUGH YOUR BLOODFLOW, LYMPHFLOW, JUICEFLOW.

FUNNING MEANS IT'S FUN OR IN-TERESTING TO LET DO. SO IS ROLLING YOUR EYES. SO IS ROLLING YOUR HEAD. SO IS WHATEVER YOU LET MOVE AND DO.   WELL DONE. NOW STOP.

This light through me really means *STOP.* He/she stops, I stop, the world stops, or so it seems. My lightness becomes more dazzling. Bliss pours through me immensely fresh and re-freshing.

ALWAYS REMEMBER TO STOP, he/she murmurs. I do remember and somehow I stop growing old too.

A SECOND VISIT TO THE LAND OF ZO

A long time afterwards and when I am thor-oughly caught in doing somethings, I suddenly stop agitating my heartflow and bloodflow. I stop exciting my nerveflow and stop jabbering my mindflow and feel myself as I ought to be.

Plop, I plop into the land and into the light-ness in the land who says at once, **NOW PAUSE.** In the land of Zo *PAUSE* always comes after *STOP.*

Pausing, *pausing,* a miracle happens. A big hole is dug before me digging itself and all my tight selfish unwise doings are being poured into this hole until I am completely free of me.

Marvelous
Stupendous.
Unbelievable.
I am between words,
before think,
even before feel
and real.
I am unstuck.

I AM ZINGING!

ZINGING I am the potential of everyone on earth and there are trillions of them, counting the plants and bugs.

THIS IS THE WAY I AM AND YOU MAY BE, he/she instructs me. **NOW BLISS THIS.** An immense *bliss* spreads through me like butter. I feel like slowly tasting icecream ought to feel. All this without taking a pill or potion.

Let me tell you too, I ever after remember to *stop* and *pause,* between words too. My old face erases and places erase into *pause* and sipping water tastes like wonder and I no longer stumble. And everything is quite all right. As said before *I ZING!*

STOP
PAUSE
this lightness
is ever with me
as me
you too.

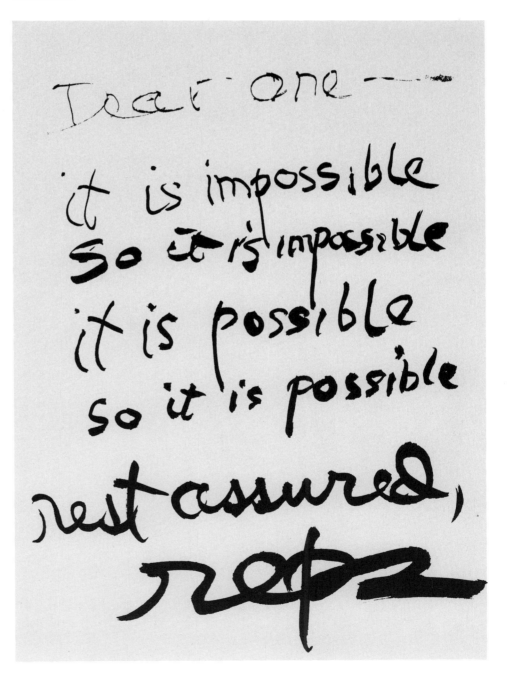

dear one———
it is impossible
so it is impossible
it is possible
so it is possible

rest assured,
reps

Since men still
        make war
Let me Lie down
    and sing
  with the grasses

I have no parents
I make heaven and earth my parents

I have no home
I make awareness my home

I have no life or death
I make breath tides my life and death

I have no divine power
I make integrity my divine power

I have no means
I make understanding my means

I have no magic secret
I make honesty my magic secret

I have no body
I make endurance my body

I have no eyes
I make the lightning flash my eyes

I have no ears
I make sensibility my ears

I have no limbs
I make promptness my limbs

I have no strategy
I make unshadowed-by-thought my strategy

I have no designs
I make opportunity my design

I have no miracles
I make right action my miracles

I have no principles
I make adaptability my principles

I have no tactics
I make emptiness/fullness my tactics

I have no friends
I make you   mind   friends

I have no enemy
I make carelessness my enemy

I have no armor
I make compassion my honor

I have no castle
I make heaven/earth my castle

I have no sword
I make absence of self my sword

—14th-century Samurai   *[from JUICING]*

The writings and drawings on the preceding three pages are taken from some of Reps' most recent work. 'Who Is' on the left is Reps' timeless masterpiece—"a whole philosophy or cosmology in a glance," he calls it.

Reps has been publishing books for over forty years, and on the following pages we present excerpts from all his books. There are traditional Zen stories from ZEN FLESH ZEN BONES, reproductions of drawings from ZEN TELEGRAMS, the entire text of his little-known classic SIT IN, selections from books still to be published, and at least a taste of all the books in between.

Many of Reps' books are now out of print and difficult to obtain. In fact, Reps rediscovered his very first book just as this book was about to go to press: "Scrounging through the library of Colorado College in Colorado Springs USA," he wrote us, "I found a book by reps published in 1939, a book you might reproduce delectably in your book on reps. Here it is!" This collection of Reps' poetry was called MORE POWER TO YOU, but Reps now likes to call it SEE SAY POEMS. We've selected some of these haiku-like poems and reproduced them on this page. What would Reps' picture poems be without the pictures? . . . .

The ant
so roughly brushed aside
still clinging to my fingers.

The pine—
drinking luminous dew
as if nothing had happened.

Thrush improvising
on telephone wire
all innocent of message within.

Turning from left to right
awakening this May morning
what unbelievable delight!

The garden grows—
intensely a gardener
pushes water from a hose.

Blockhead!
Pointing at the moon
when asked the way to town.

Loafing in sun
eating grass
not so poor.

Passing in the hot street
once and forever
we—knowing—smile.

Sitting on a tack
I am instantly
center of the universe.

Half-drowned sand-sodden bee
whirring in frenzy
crawls towards the sea.

Motionless on a rock
squirrel in bright wonder
measuring surveyor.

Waves—waves—waves
and deep below
none come—none go.

Earthworm, lover of roots
though cut in two
returning.

Again and again
that fellow's web
over the cellar-door keyhole.

Two identical then chaos—
this white night
of drifting flakes.

Bubbling ice-edged spring—
neither can words
measure our heart's tide.

[*In the introduction to* ZEN FLESH, ZEN BONES *Reps cautions the reader: "Old Zen was so fresh it became treasured and remembered. Here are fragments of its skin, flesh, bones, but not its marrow—never found in words." And so this book serves many as their first taste of Zen.*

Reps transcribed these Zen writings with Nyogen Senzaki in the 1930's, and published separately 101 ZEN STORIES, THE GATELESS GATE, *and* 10 BULLS. *Charles Tuttle Co. published all three in one volume twenty years later, and we present excerpts below. Reps still asks us, "Dare we open our doors to the source of our being? What are flesh and bones for?"*]

From 101 ZEN STORIES

A Cup of Tea

Nan-in, a Japanese master during the Meiji era (1868–1912), received a university professor who came to inquire about Zen. Nan-in served tea. He poured his visitor's cup full, and then kept on pouring.

The professor watched the overflow until he no longer could restrain himself. "It is overfull. No more will go in!"

"Like this cup," Nan-in said, "you are full of your own opinions and speculations. How can I show you Zen unless you first empty your cup?"

Is That So?

The Zen master Hakuin was praised by his neighbors as one living a pure life. A beautiful Japanese girl whose parents owned a food store lived near him. Suddenly, without any warning, her parents discovered she was with child. This made her parents angry. She would not confess who the man was, but after much harassment at last named Hakuin.

In great anger the parents went to the master. "Is that so?" was all he would say.

After the child was born it was brought to Hakuin. By this time he had lost his reputation, which did not trouble him, but he took very good care of the child. He obtained milk from his neighbors and everything else the little one needed. A year later the girl-mother could stand it no longer. She told her parents the truth—that the real father of the child was a young man who worked in the fishmarket. The mother and father of the girl at once went to Hakuin to ask his forgiveness, to apologize at length, and to get the child back again.

Hakuin was willing. In yielding the child, all he said was: "Is that so?"

Muddy Road

Tanzan and Ekido were once traveling together down a muddy road. A heavy rain was still falling. Coming around a bend, they met a lovely girl in a silk kimono and sash, unable to cross the intersection.

"Come on, girl," said Tanzan at once. Lifting her in his arms, he carried her over the mud.

Ekido did not speak again until that night when they reached a lodging temple. Then he no longer could restrain himself. "We monks don't go near females," he told Tanzan, "especially not young and lovely ones. It is dangerous. Why did you do that?"

"I left the girl there," said Tanzan. "Are you still carrying her?"

A Parable

Buddha told a parable in a sutra:

A man traveling across a field encountered a tiger. He fled, the tiger after him. Coming to a precipice, he caught hold of the root of a wild vine and swung himself down over the edge. The tiger sniffed at him from above. Trembling, the man looked down to where, far below, another tiger was waiting to eat him. Only the vine sustained him.

Two mice, one white and one black, little by little started to gnaw away the vine. The man saw a luscious strawberry near him. Grasping the vine with one hand, he plucked the strawberry with the other. How sweet it tasted!

The First Principle

When one goes to Obaku temple in Kyoto he sees carved over the gate the words "The First Principle." The letters are unusually large, and those who appreciate calligraphy always admire them as being a masterpiece. They were drawn by Kosen two hundred years ago.

When the master drew them he did so on paper, from which workmen made the larger carving in wood. As Kosen sketched the letters a bold pupil was with him who had made several gallons of ink for the calligraphy and who never failed to criticize his master's work.

"That is not good," he told Kosen after the first effort.

"How is that one?"

"Poor. Worse than before," pronounced the pupil.

Kosen patiently wrote one sheet after another until eighty-four First Principles had accumulated, still without the approval of the pupil.

Then, when the young man stepped outside for a few moments, Kosen thought: "Now is my chance to escape his keen eye," and he wrote hurriedly, with a mind free from distraction: "The First Principle."

"A masterpiece," pronounced the pupil.

Eating the Blame

Circumstances arose one day which delayed preparation of the dinner of a Soto Zen master, Fugai, and his followers. In haste the cook went to the garden with his curved knife and cut off the tops of green vegetables, chopped them together, and made soup, unaware that in his haste he had included a part of a snake in the vegetables.

The followers of Fugai thought they never had tasted such good soup. But when the master himself found the snake's head in his bowl, he summoned the cook. "What is this?" he demanded, holding up the head of the snake.

"Oh, thank you, master," replied the cook, taking the morsel and eating it quickly.

Nothing Exists

Yamaoka Tesshu, as a young student of Zen, visited one master after another. He called upon Dokuon of Shokoku. Desiring to show his attainment, he said: "The mind, Buddha, and sentient beings, after all, do not exist. The true nature of phenomena is emptiness. There is no realization, no delusion, no sage, no mediocrity. There is no giving and nothing to be received."

Dokuon, who was smoking quietly, said nothing. Suddenly he whacked Yamaoka with his bamboo pipe. This made the youth quite angry.

"If nothing exists," inquired Dokuon, "where did this anger come from?"

Publishing the Sutras

Tetsugen, a devotee of Zen in Japan, decided to publish the sutras, which at that time were available only in Chinese. The books were to be printed with wood blocks in an edition of seven thousand copies, a tremendous undertaking.

Tetsugen began by traveling and collecting donations for this purpose. A few sympathizers would give him a hundred pieces of gold, but most of the time he received only small coins. He thanked each donor with equal gratitude. After ten years Tetsugen had enough money to begin his task.

It happened that at that time the Uji River overflowed. Famine followed. Tetsugen took the funds he had collected for the books and spent them to save others from starvation. Then he began again his work of collecting.

Several years afterwards an epidemic spread over the country. Tetsugen again gave away what he had collected, to help his people.

For a third time he started his work, and after twenty years his wish was fulfilled. The printing blocks which produced the first edition of sutras can be seen today in the Obaku monastery in Kyoto.

The Japanese tell their children that Tetsugen made three sets of sutras, and that the first two invisible sets surpass even the last.

Joshu's Zen

Joshu began the study of Zen when he was sixty years old and continued until he was eighty, when he realized Zen. He taught from the age of eighty until he was one hundred and twenty. A student once asked him: "If I haven't anything in my mind, what shall I do?"

Joshu replied: "Throw it out."

"But if I haven't anything, how can I throw it out?" continued the questioner.

"Well," said Joshu, "then carry it out."

No Work, No Food

Hyakujo, the Chinese Zen master, used to labor with his pupils even at the age of eighty, trimming the gardens, cleaning the grounds, and pruning the trees. The pupils felt sorry to see the old teacher working so hard, but they knew he would not listen to their advice to stop, so they hid away his tools.

That day the master did not eat. The next day he did not eat, nor the next. "He may be angry because we have hidden his tools," the pupils surmised. "We had better put them back." The day they did, the teacher worked and ate the same as before. In the evening he instructed them: "No work, no food."

Three Days More

Suiwo, the disciple of Hakuin, was a good teacher. During one summer seclusion period, a pupil came to him from a southern island of Japan.

Suiwo gave him the problem: "Hear the sound of one hand."

The pupil remained three years but could not pass this test. One night he came in tears to Suiwo. "I must return south in shame and embarrassment," he said, "for I cannot solve my problem."

"Wait one week more and meditate constantly," advised Suiwo. Still no enlightenment came to the pupil. "Try for another week," said Suiwo. The pupil obeyed, but in vain.

Still another week. Yet this was of no avail. In despair the student begged to be released, but Suiwo requested another meditation of five days. They were without result. Then he said: "Meditate for three days longer, then if you fail to attain enlightenment, you had better kill yourself."

On the second day the pupil was enlightened.

From THE GATELESS GATE

Buddha Twirls a Flower

When Buddha was in Grdhrakuta mountain he turned a flower in his fingers and held it before his listeners. Every one was silent. Only Maha-Kashapa smiled at this revelation, although he tried to control the lines of his face.

Buddha said: "I have the eye of the true teaching, the heart of Nirvana, the true aspect of non-form, and the ineffable stride of Dharma. It is not expressed by words, but especially transmitted beyond teaching. This teaching I have given to Maha-Kashapa."

Mumon's comment: Golden-faced Gautama thought he could cheat anyone. He made the good listeners as bad, and sold dog meat under the sign of mutton. And he himself thought it was wonderful. What if all the audience had laughed together? How could he have transmitted the teaching? And again, if Maha-Kashapa had not smiled, how could he have transmitted the teaching? If he says that realization can be transmitted, he is like the city slicker that cheats the country dub, and if he says it cannot be transmitted, why does he approve of Maha-Kashapa?

At the turning of a flower
His disguise was exposed.
No one in heaven or earth can surpass
Maha-Kashapa's wrinkled face.

Joshu's Dog

A monk asked Joshu, a Chinese Zen master: "Has a dog Buddha-nature or not?"

Joshu answered: "Mu." [Mu is the negative symbol in Chinese, meaning "No thing" or "Nay."]

Mumon's comment: To realize Zen one has to pass through the barrier of the patriarchs. Enlightenment always comes after the road of thinking is blocked. If you do not pass the barrier of the patriarchs or if your thinking road is not blocked, whatever you think, whatever you do, is like a tangling ghost. You may ask: What is a barrier of a patriarch? This one word, Mu, is it.

This is the barrier of Zen. If you pass through it you will see Joshu face to face. Then you can work hand in hand with the whole line of patriarchs. Is this not a pleasant thing to do?

If you want to pass this barrier, you must work through every bone in your body, through every pore of your skin, filled with this question: What is Mu? and carry it day and night. Do not believe it is the common negative symbol meaning nothing. It is not nothingness, the opposite of existence. If you really want to pass this barrier, you should feel like drinking a hot iron ball that you can neither swallow nor spit out.

Then your previous lesser knowledge disappears. As a fruit ripening in season, your subjectivity and objectivity naturally become one. It is like a dumb man who has had a dream. He knows about it but he cannot tell it.

When he enters this condition his ego-shell is crushed and he can shake the heaven and move the earth. He is like a great warrior with a sharp sword. If a Buddha stands in his way, he will cut him down; if a patriarch offers him any obstacle, he will kill him; and he will be free in his way of birth and death. He can enter any world as if it were his own playground. I will tell you how to do this with this koan:

Just concentrate your whole energy into this Mu, and do not allow any discontinuation. When you enter this Mu and there is no discontinuation, your attainment will be as a candle burning and illuminating the whole universe.

Has a dog Buddha-nature?
This is the most serious question of all.
If you say yes or no,
You lose your own Buddha-nature.

Bells and Robes

Ummon asked: "The world is such a wide world, why do you answer a bell and don ceremonial robes?"

Mumon's comment: When one studies Zen one need not follow sound or color or form. Even though some have attained insight when hearing a voice or seeing a color or a form, this is a very common way. It is not true Zen. The real Zen student controls sound, color, form, and actualizes the truth in his everyday life.

Sound comes to the ear, the ear goes to sound. When you blot out sound and sense, what do you understand? While listening with ears one never can understand. To understand intimately one should see sound.

When you understand, you belong to the family,
When you do not understand, you are a stranger.
Those who do not understand belong to the family,
And when they understand they are strangers.

It Is Not Mind, It Is Not Buddha, It Is Not Things

A monk asked Nansen: "Is there a teaching no master ever preached before?"

Nansen said: "Yes, there is."

"What is it?" asked the monk.

Nansen replied: "It is not mind, it is not Buddha, it is not things."

Mumon's comment: Old Nansen gave away his treasure-words. He must have been greatly upset.

Nansen was too kind and lost his treasure.
Truly, words have no power.
Even though the mountain becomes the sea,
Words cannot open another's mind.

An Oak Tree in the Garden

A monk asked Joshu why Bodhidharma came to China.

Joshu said: "An oak tree in the garden."

Mumon's comment: If one sees Joshu's answer clearly, there is no Shakyamuni Buddha before him and no future Buddha after him.

Words cannot describe everything.
The Heart's message cannot be delivered in words.
If one receives words literally, he will be lost,
If he tries to explain with words, he will not attain enlightenment in this life.

Ummon's Sidetrack

A Zen student told Ummon: "Brilliancy of Buddha illuminates the whole universe."

Before he finished the phrase Ummon asked: "You are reciting another's poem, are you not?"

"Yes," answered the student.

"You are sidetracked," said Ummon.

Afterwards another teacher, Shishin, asked his pupils: "At what point did that student go off the track?"

Mumon's comment: If anyone perceives Ummon's particular skillfulness, he will know at what point the student was off the track, and he will be a teacher of man and Devas. If not, he cannot even perceive himself.

When a fish meets the fishhook
If he is too greedy, he will be caught.
When his mouth opens
His life already is lost.

Bodhidharma Pacifies the Mind

Bodhidharma sits facing the wall. His future successor stands in the snow and presents his severed arm to Bodhidharma. He cries: "My mind is not pacified. Master, pacify my mind."

Bodhidharma says: "If you bring me that mind, I will pacify it for you."

The successor says: "When I search my mind I cannot hold it."

Bodhidharma says: Then your mind is pacified already."

Mumon's comment: That broken-toothed old Hindu, Bodhidharma, came thousands of miles over the sea from India to China as if he had something wonderful. He is like raising waves without wind. After he remained years in China he had only one disciple and that one lost his arm and was deformed. Alas, ever since he has had brainless disciples.

Why did Bodhidharma come to China?
For years monks have discussed this.
All the troubles that have followed since
Came from that teacher and disciple.

From 10 BULLS

The Search for the Bull

In the pasture of this world, I endlessly push aside the tall grasses in search of the bull.

Following unnamed rivers, lost upon the interpenetrating paths of distant mountains, My strength failing and my vitality exhausted, I cannot find the bull.

I only hear the locusts chirring through the forest at night.

Comment: The bull never has been lost. What need is there to search? Only because of separation from my true nature, I fail to find him. In the confusion of the senses I lose even his tracks. Far from home, I see many crossroads, but which way is the right one I know not. Greed and fear, good and bad, entangle me.

Discovering the Footprints

Along the riverbank under the trees, I discover footprints!

Even under the fragrant grass I see his prints.

Deep in remote mountains they are found.

These traces no more can be hidden than one's nose, looking heavenward.

Comment: Understanding the teaching, I see the footprints of the bull. Then I learn that, just as many utensils are made from one metal, so too are myriad entities made of the fabric of self. Unless I discriminate, how will I perceive the true from the untrue? Not yet having entered the gate, nevertheless I have discerned the path.

Perceiving the Bull

I hear the song of the nightingale.

The sun is warm, the wind is mild, willows are green along the shore,

Here no bull can hide!

What artist can draw that massive head, those majestic horns?

Comment: When one hears the voice, one can sense its source, As soon as the six senses merge, the gate is entered. Wherever one enters one sees the head of the bull! This unity is like salt in water, like color in dyestuff. The slightest thing is not apart from self.

Catching the Bull

I seize him with a terrific struggle.

His great will and power are inexhaustible.

He charges to the high plateau far above the cloud-mists,

Or in an impenetrable ravine he stands.

Comment: He dwelt in the forest a long time, but I caught him today! Infatuation for scenery interferes with his direction. Longing for sweeter grass, he wanders away. His mind still is stubborn and unbridled. If I wish him to submit, I must raise my whip.

Taming the Bull

The whip and rope are necessary

Else he might stray off down some dusty road.

Being well trained, he becomes naturally gentle.

Then, unfettered, he obeys his master.

Comment: When one thought arises, another thought follows. When the first thought springs from enlightenment, all subsequent thoughts are true. Through delusion, one makes everything untrue. Delusion is not caused by objectivity; it is the result of subjectivity. Hold the nose-ring tight and do not allow even a doubt.

Riding the Bull Home

Mounting the bull, slowly I return homeward.

The voice of my flute intones through the evening.

Measuring with hand-beats the pulsating harmony, I direct the endless rhythm.

Whoever hears this melody will join me.

Comment: This struggle is over; gain and loss are assimilated. I sing the song of the village woodsman, and play the tunes of the children. Astride the bull, I observe the clouds above. Onward I go, no matter who may wish to call me back.

The Bull Transcended

Astride the bull, I reach home.

I am serene. The bull too can rest.

The dawn has come. In blissful repose,

Within my thatched dwelling I have abandoned the whip and rope.

Comment: All is one law, not two. We only make the bull a temporary subject. It is as the relation of rabbit and trap, of fish and net. It is as gold and dross, or the moon emerging from a cloud. One path of clear light travels on throughout endless time.

Both Bull and Self Transcended

Whip, rope, person, and bull—all merge in No-Thing.

This heaven is so vast no message can stain it.

How may a snowflake exist in a raging fire?

Here are the footprints of the patriarchs.

Comment: Mediocrity is gone. Mind is clear of limitation. I seek no state of enlightenment. Neither do I remain where no enlightenment exists. Since I linger in neither condition, eyes cannot see me. If hundreds of birds strew my path with flowers, such praise would be meaningless.

Reaching the Source

Too many steps have been taken returning to the root and the source.

Better to have been blind and deaf from the beginning!

Dwelling in one's true abode, unconcerned with that without—

The river flows tranquilly on and the flowers are red.

Comment: From the beginning, truth is clear. Poised in silence, I observe the forms of integration and disintegration. One who is not attached to "form" need not be "reformed." The water *is* emerald, the mountain *is* indigo, and I see that which *is* creating and that which *is* destroying.

In the World

Barefooted and naked of breast, I mingle with the people of the world

My clothes are ragged and dust-laden, and I am ever blissful.

I use no magic to extend my life;

Now, before me, the dead trees become alive.

Comment: Inside my gate, a thousand sages do not know me. The beauty of my garden is invisible. Why should one search for the footprints of the patriarchs? I go to the market place with my wine bottle and return home with my staff. I visit the wineshop and the market, and everyone I look upon becomes enlightened.

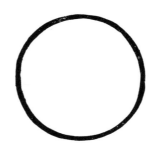

"Friend, dare we unknot in these troubling times? Must we compound strife with us? Can we invite one person, ourself, into organic harmony? If your answer is 'yes', this makes you a member in good standing of the unknotting group in your world, a portion of the unknotting brotherhood that must flower from the soil of turmoil.   It entitles you to share the beauty of plant and flower, the harmony of animals, the love of little children and good feeling of beings everywhere."

[From the introduction to UNKNOT THE WORLD IN YOU*]*

UNOBSTRUCTED, HEAD TO FEET

Let's start with our head.
RELEASE LINES
IN FOREHEAD.
GRADUALLY RELEASE
LINES IN FACE.
RELEASE EYE NERVES
FAR INTO HEAD
AND THROUGHOUT
UNTIL YOU SEEM TO FILL
WITH SOFT LIGHT.

Let this inner seed-light through. Call it light, creativity, lucidity—but have the experience.
LET HEAD FLOAT
STRAIGHT UP
FROM THE CENTER OF
THE LIVING EARTH.
DON'T PUSH IT.
LET IT FLOAT UP, UP.

To do this you do nothing.

Being an adult carries weight. Floating relieves the heaviness. Beginning in head, it becomes a total experience.

How many moments of the day do you force and how many do you float? A struggling swimmer sinks. A floater enjoys the ocean.

The eyes!
BLINK ONCE
AS BREATH FLOWS IN.

With any of our 50,000 picture-taking blinks daily, we both see and unsee. The blink and you are never apart. Actualize this. As you do so you find you are no longer distracted, divided, lost, but attentively all here. It feels good to blink and you stop troubling for a flash. What a simple way into ease!
SEE SOME OBJECT AT EYE LEVEL.
CLOSING EYES,
GRADUALLY LET THE OBJECT GO.
OPENING EYES,
SEE IT APPEAR SOFTLY—
ITS VOLUME, COLOR, URGE.

What is outsight? What we see.
What is insight? How we see.

Our ears!
PULL BOTH EARLOBES
DOWN SLIGHTLY.

Ears like to be stretched occasionally. How do sounds affect us? In ways we interpret them. Each sound wakes new responses in us. Freshly, listen to drip of distant water, rustle of wind through grass. We can almost hear their beauty.

The nose!
OPEN NOSTRILS,
LETTING THEM EXPAND
WITH INBREATHS.
PULL THEM DOWNWARD
WITH THUMBS AND FOREFINGERS
TO STRAIGHTEN THE NOSE.

As hard lines in face release, oxygen intake increases.

The mouth!
A SMILE TONICS

A face gets set. A smile unsets it. As hard lines in face release, our past and future difficulties smooth out. We naturally smile as they smooth, and they naturally smooth as we smile.

The neck!
Our neck tells us how we are this hour. Delicate nervestuff flows neckward from brainstem to sacral plexus and into glands and organs. Whatever we do registers at once in this invisible lifestream. Try to turn over in bed without tightening the neck. We live miserably as we stiffen through the neck, often without knowing it. To live well, we soften it.
INTIMATELY TELL IT
"LET GO, NECK."
TELL IT KINDLY.
THEN DO NOTHING.

Every part of us likes such guidance and will respond unexpectedly. Babies and sages show us the rapturous art of the soft neck. Who ever saw a baby with a tight neck? A gently flowing neck soothes our central nerves, head and spine, and alerts our appreciations. As we look, walk, exert, without tightening the neck, vital fluids from brain and base merge in heart. We live in bliss.

The middle!
Here we register and store even a parent's or grandparents's tensions until as our own we transform them. Why do we register them? Because we imitate. Because as we grow up we forget to bend down, to jump for joy, to contract and release totally. Because we don't move as a whole. Because we live possessively instead of spontaneously with others.

These localized stresses cement into muscle groups and wait for us to release them. We may have resorted to foods, to drink, to stimulants, to entertainments, in vain. We may have travelled far or changed companions. We may have relaxed inertly or been relaxed by others only to wrap ourselves in the old knots afterwards. Sooner or later

we see WE are responsible. This facing ourself, seemingly the hardest thing to do, becomes the easiest.
GRADUALLY TENSE
EVERY MIDDLE MUSCLE.
THEN EASE, EASE
THE ENTIRE MIDDLE.

How simple! What can we lose but the old strictures, the old binds? Visceral fears disappear and unbending restraints vanish.

The arms!
We overtense shoulders and neglect to release them.
FIRMLY WE TELL THEM
Let go, shoulders.
Let go, elbows.
Let go, good hands.
WE LET THEM.

Loose hands make for loose wrists. Loose wrists subtract elbow restraints. Loose-swinging straight arms comfort the shoulders. As shoulders loosen, much world troubling untroubles.

The legs!
Cramps in legs stop at once by pulling the toes up as far as possible toward the knees.
PAD SOFTLY WHEN WALKING
WALK UNSTIFFLEGGED.

Flex knees, legs swinging straight ahead, not toeing out, to get us there. Stroll behind someone flexible to see how they do it.

Good feet!
Our feet, much used and little thanked, support us. How? With inner direction.
LIE DOWN AND
PUT YOUR WHOLE ATTENTION
IN YOUR FEET.

As you do this a warm glow of circulation spreads through them. Our feet should be alive as our hands. Feeling them moving, then unmoving. Yet "feet" and "we" are one. "Head", "middle", "feet", cannot be detached from us. We act as one through them.
FEEL FEET
TIRED, TIRED.
NOW FEEL THEM
LIGHT AS FEATHERS.

In feeling through feet and all of us, we are making our future right now. Our feet belong on earth, our head in the sun.

 [ZEN TELEGRAMS. *An art show bound into book form intended to be unbound by the reader. "I call them all 'telegrams' . . . a combination of ink lines and telegraphic prose."*

The story is told of a man entering a hospital who, when asked his religion, replied "Zen Buddhist." No Zen Buddhist monk came to visit him as he convalesced, but a wise friend sent him a copy of ZEN TELEGRAMS. *The man got well.*

A collection of "zen telegrams" follows.]

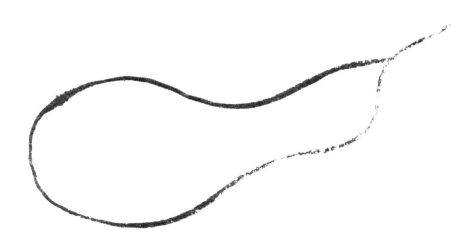

cucumber
unaccountably
cucumbering

though
wide the sky
never lost
wild geese
cry

how to
be
a
samurai

ants
how thankful
I am
with no thing
to be thankful
for

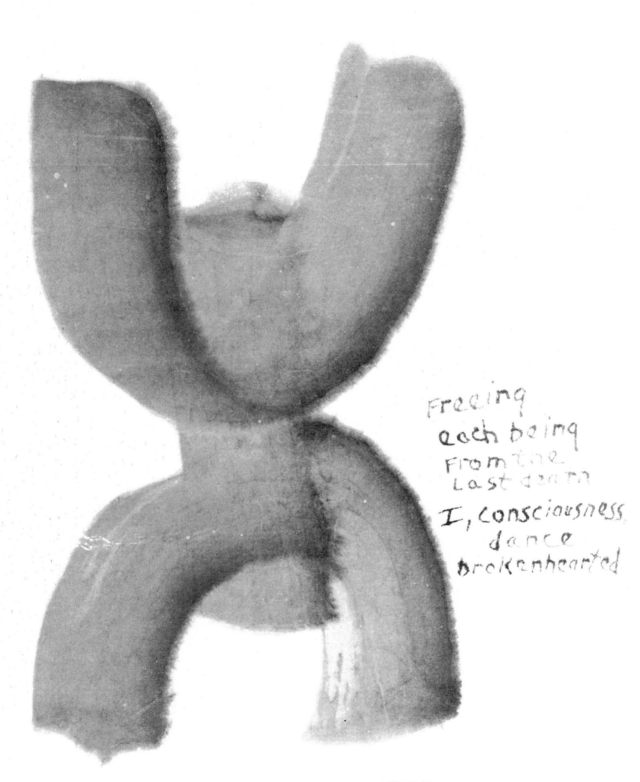

Freeing
each being
from the
Last death

I, consciousness
dance
Brokenhearted

"*STOP. Reverse on go—by reading this book backwards Chinese style, right to left, day-night. (Back up may be a poetic experience.) Each poem stands by itself.*

The red seals are for red—a drop of lifeblood. Over Japan and other places reps gives in-visible in-soundable poems, one to one. A Kyoto poet first gathered them into a 'show' in Kyoto.

Find some long bamboo. String-tie together as child's space house. Tape poems at top to bamboo like washing. Let the wind blow. Look. IN-look."

[*From the introduction to* BIG BATH]

breaking the
Light barrier

"Bill—Had my horrorscope read yesterday, Chinese way, says big fame in 1963. GOLD/FISH is terrific—life plus love or consideration.

My Hongkong publisher, a famous calligrapher who supplies me seals, and others all met by chance, and this impossible if I hadn't sat down in a store and had time to loaf and talk and enjoy. If someone had been with me it couldn't have happened. Girl with me in Japan down street in Nagano city I simply deserted to walk into fish store where I found gyotaku. She tagged in later to translate. Man must be man, supposes   reps."

Fish Like
no
dish

POEMIC SIGNATURES OF FISH

After wandering the Japan Alps I came to Nagano City. Something led me quickly into a store for fishermen. Being one of the countless persons who prefers to admire rather than to catch fish, I wondered why.

High up on the walls *gyotaku* were displayed. These are rubbings of the forms of fish as Japanese have done them for centuries. They are made by brushing the fish on one side with *sumi* (black ink), then pressing with rice paper. Fish leaves his signature on the paper.

The man and wife who displayed these with fish equipment were specialists. The husband caught the fish. The wife helped with the impress and often gave the fish away, not wishing to kill it. Detail of the kind, size, weight, place, day, and weather condition appeared as a kind of remembrance of the event.

A fish can live two hours out of water, we can live but two minutes out of air. Directions for making the signature:

BORROW FISH
BRUSH WITH *SUMI*
PRESS WITH PAPER
BATHE FISH
RETURN TO WATER

In Kyoto I borrowed some fish from a fishmonger's tank and made a few fish signatures. The more excited the subject, the more difficult to get a detailed impress but one where the fish moves looks more startling than one taken from a passive swimmer. When he splotches his signature with a shrug or twist it gives a recording of motion. Perhaps the *sumi* ink tickles.

Fish seemed to me to intuit what was going on, squirming and then resting in my hands in a kind of momentary faith, knowing he would return to water. I was shocked to feel the fish exercising a sense underneath intuition or knowing.

Fish care nothing for publicity, honor or immortality on these pages. It is a life or death matter to be taken out of one's element into deadly air. The signature had better be made on the bank of a stream where a pro-fish *gyotaku* maker might ask the fisherman to spare a life out of loving kindness.

Fish shows us vividly that our actual home is in air rather than in New York, Tokyo, Madras, Moscow. Can our death to them from sewage and chemical dumping and water pollution come back to us in smoke-smog-bomb polluted air? By accident, war, old age, we too may be lifted out of our layer of air unexpectedly.

Inconsideration is worse than death. For our own good we need consideration of fish more than of dish. Our lack of poemic feel registers in outworn political prose wherein we put an end, a period, to sentences. We sentence ourself.

Our need to think in new symbolisms is urgent. Perhaps fish who knows no end can help us. Motion is such a language, poetry another.

The notion came to me to put down what I have learned with fish. Some of these compressions arise. When drawn lines accompany them I call them picture-poems but they only imply rhythm, are unpolished, brief as slang, as if the words jumped out, and are to be completed by you.

Outside and inside of Japan people are going to fast these days to read overlong print. Anything worth saying can be said on a postcard or in a telegram or breath-blown. My *says* compact in poemic telegrams.

So now I have a live fish, its action in hand, its naked signature, joy of return to water, eye impress, its silent sound and lines on rice paper. My fish or word is second-hand dead. Better become *Fish* instead.

"*A millionaire flower in Mexico asks me to his home. 'Tell us one of your poems.' I do.*

Cucumber
unaccountably
cucumbering

'That's no poem,' he angers, 'you may as well say peony peonying.' Is it so far from plant to poem? Animals and children experience pre-experience. Why decorate, necktie and high-heel it? I don't know too."

[*From the preface to* PICTURE POEM PRIMER]

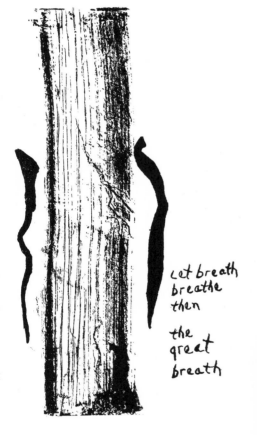

let breath
breathe
then

the
great
breath

We experience something then explain it. Explaining we get second-hand. Before conceiving. Before outing (into this and that) we are here. Lightpoints package us, unborning mostly, a smallest portion of us showing. It takes a thousand suns to make a man. And one seed.

Even the winged insect knows the way

Walk in breath. Integrity lets the actual great breath through, both nostrils clear, breath insinging 24,000 sea-with sky-with breaths each 24 (h) ours.
Dare I in-vite this radiant welling?

Nervestream compressing-celebrating in exquisite slow dovelove rhythm 15 a minute opening flowerlikely luminously nectar distilling head to heart.
Morning mist over leafing tree
just sitting still   still
Everyone a Buddha

Day-night, try-let, squeeze-open are for us. A legend tells how creator created a world by "Tzim-Tzum" squeezing substance and light out of.

To enter sound and motion, to enter sound and motion, to enter mind ocean, right now . . .
Sound of flowing water
motion of birch leaves
any sound, any motion our examination.
Longlived Sufis inbreathe the heart sound Ugl-lah, outbreathe "hoo" over heart with a circular head motion gently waking all this in love as a child in mother. We breathe us into heart.

Standing in the rain we are for e v e r something-ness some thingness transmiting.
Pebble, twig, bush, frog, human, overhuman, no two
the same, unique, incomparable . . . one.

Standing
in the rain
sitting in the sun
isn't it wonderful

Has fly more I than I?
Fragrancing high, higher, into the 1
Prison bars melt. We are children playing. Fortunate, what we will say in the next minute surprises. Whoever makes claims stiffens.

Nature lives this poem. So does cat, the meditator, sinuous, soft, sharp, flexive, independent, in-motion, so audibly purring.
Music guides our deep attention. Our mind, our attention follows tone. A finest oil for a finest instrument? In-tone. Troubling only tries to be out of harmony.
Easy sit, up, some silent word in attention (as "whoo", growing sound) Listen in this core vibration toward the only be-ing.

We are fast constructing a one-world out-lighted electromagnetic society that can do everything but bud. Electric with force, soon magnetic force-free to take us out there—and in here?

Nobly considerately Amerindians have a way for a need to be filled in great nature.
Facing East, open arms and ask
(our first parent) for what is needed.
Place hands over middle.
Do so in turn South, West, North.
Facing East, receive. Share it.

In sleep-dream-wake why not 'ask' for the big wake. Why? To accord. Out of accord we desperately need food for the hungry and shelter for the homeless, needs not yet met because we are confused, turned in on ourself, missing ways to turn in for others, to welcome all good possibilities.

We turn water to wine, helping another, inventing letters and numbers from shapes and cell rhythms, in-venting these tubes for flow, expansively yesing heartstream good.

The show goes on in our mind of mind, already free, spacious, includingly. If we only think, if we think we are unfree we are out of our mind. Here, bright. Black Flower fragrancing. Bird ultrasounding. Sure as bud.
Thrush: Don't stop here.
Why not live in-finitely?

buddings

7 Feb 64

Dear Bill

    Anyway Cora will love it
and I love it
and I hope you will like it

it is just what it says a primer
and I have seen the first copy
and maybe in a day or more one will be airmailed to you
and I hope you like it too

and Liu says maybe 3,000 will be done before the Chinese
New Year
justifying his longtime trust in his publisher printer Lee
and the rest 3 weeks after they stop celebrating

even those who owe money can shows their faces New Years
Day and not get dunned

Liu is one of us, but young, lithe
and for me the book vibrates his careful enthusiastic
dear supervision overlooking its detail

it has a few minor errors you may miss on reading
as we did but these make the book still more human

and the point is in a short time, maybe a year
no one will be able to get a hand-bound book such as this
of Gold/ fish signatures
as the labor simply will not work doing it any more
except at exorbitant cost

so our 25¢ cost is a kind of little miracle, thanks to Liu Jimmy

Chinese, old days, often did books for their friends
and this is one, a knife as a Japanese says of it
yet apparently modest all through

it's just lovely
so please take off your careful printing scruples
and have a look at a really handmade book

and I'm trying to autograph them all and Liu is trying
to put a red seal on them all and I bot ink for the red
seal that he says won't turn dull in 500 years
whereas on so many old Chinese paintings the seals have
darkened
and he has taken out insurance on the books against fire
with an insurance Co. Japanese who are his friends
so if the whole undelivered lot of them should burn
your money would be protected
now isn't that just wonderful !!!!!

[They may seem odd these plays. Everyday life unwrinkled. The movements, the thoughts, the words of rocks, flowers, animals and men unwrinkled. And then opposite each play is a brushstroke poem, unwrinkling the words themselves in a glance.

One of the plays is a four line conversation between a woman and child: (**Child:** *Where am I?* **Woman:** *Dear child, you are being born here.* **Child:** *Let me out.* **Woman:** *Let yourself out*).

Were these plays meant to be performed on the real-life stage? "If they exist in the mind of the reader," says Reps, "then they are on the real-life stage."]

GOAT LIFE

Sheep (*Going to market, to a goat*): What will become of me?
Goat (*going to market*): They will eat you.
Sheep: I want to eat, not to be eaten. Will they eat you too?
Goat: They will, but I shall pierce them with my horns.

The scene changes to one foul and bloody.

Man: Come here, sheep. No one lives forever. (Slits its throat)
Sheep (*to goat*): Pierce them!
Goat (*as its throat is slit*): Death eater, eat my death.

The sheep who is no longer a sheep awakes. The goat who is no longer a goat awakes. The man who is no longer a man awakes.

Sheep: It was a dream.
Goat: A horror.
Man: Forgive me.
Sheep: You are forgiven.
Goat: What is there to forgive in a nightmare?
Man: Forgive me in the nightmare.
Goat: Forget it.
Man: I can't.
Sheep: Since, again, you shall be sheep and I a man who slits your throat. And goat, what shall you be?
Goat: Waking from a bad dream why go back into it? Let's be what passes all imagination.
Sheep: A man who loves?
Man: Some yet greater being?
Goat: You two are still dreaming. You have wool and knife in mind. Shall we be what we always have been always will be?

OPERATION

A Doctor's Office. Woman radiantly healthy enters with her sick self moving in consonance with her.
Woman: This doesn't smell like a doctor's office.
Thin Man: (*enters led by his sick self*): I seem to have been led here.
Nurse enters with her sick self. The nurse, woman, and sick man do not notice their sick selves.
Nurse: The doctor will see you soon.
Doctor enters. The three sick selves hurriedly pick up medicines, drugs, pills, surgical instruments, giving them to the doctor, urging him to treat their well selves. He does so.
Woman (*with an appealing glance at the thin man*): I only wanted to use the ladies' room.
Thin Man (*as medicine is forced on him*): I am looking for a plumber.
Nurse: The doctor will see you soon.
Doctor: Go home and rest. Everything will be all right.
The three sick selves push the doctor to a couch, forcing medicines on him. Assisted by the nurse, they begin to operate.
Doctor (*just before the incision*): There's nothing wrong with me!

VILLAGERS

Earth has become a village of many colors.
Negro: Night breathes us out, day breathes us in.
American: I don't know about that. We make machines to fill any man's need.
Chinese: And overfill. We need emptying along with things.
Indian: We need God, India always has said and searched.
Moslem: Our need is Allah, presently.
Eskimo: What are these strange names? Haven't we eyes to see, ears to hear the silent word?
Negro: We hear.
Chinese: The word is us.
Indian: Let us chant it together in our night-day dream.
Moslem: Agreed.
Eskimo: With bear, seal, porpoise, penguin.
American: Friend, you would go backward, we to world constructs.
Indian: We have gone to many worlds and without machines.
Moslem: Worlds, worlds, specks in Allah's eye, sighs in his sight.
Chinese: We are villagers, remember this.
Japanese: Bamboo rustles without wind.
Negro: May I sing the aliving word for you?

UPSTREAMING

This play is produced in less than a week.
A river. Summer.
A man stands waist-high in the water, facing upstream.
He stands there all day
Indrinking earth and air.
He is there the next day.
Villagers notice him.
A young woman ventures to bring him some brown rice.
He accepts it without changing position.
Others join him.
Some philosophers come to confer on the bank without
Entering the water.
Scientists take the river's temperature and
Decide the man exemplifies some profound truth
Or other. They name it upstreaming.
News of this spreads.
People come from far away to stand in the river.
They enjoy it.
No one talks,
The water is cool,
The wind like wine.
It is good to be barefoot
And to look into sky.

SEED

Seed:
Let's
be
a
tree.
Tree:
Let's
be
a
seed.

"I went to the library one day and discovered the European philosophers. And while I was reading these, a white-haired man who was head of the library came up and dropped the Bhagavad Gita and the Upanishads in front of me. So I decided to go to India and see what kind of nation produced this inner philosophy. I got a job on a boat and worked my way to India. When I got there I soon went deep into the Himalayas where the tigers roared every night, and began to live as they lived there."

[*So Reps began to wander in the early 1900's.* SQUARE SUN SQUARE MOON *is a collection of "sweet and sour essays" from his worldwide travels.*]

SWEET SOUR SALIVA TO YOUNG
A CHINESE METHOD OF LONG LIFE

there really is a bao che man at 508 chatham road, kowloon hongkong — much respected by his people for his skill in the chinese healing arts. he sends his sea-shell powder to friends over the world. he does not have a long silver beard.

Among the Chinese it is well known that the ground powder of sea pearl keeps people from growing old.

Actors and actresses take it, many rich persons. It is too costly for the common people who often see their noted ones looking as if they were 30 at 60. They attribute it at least in part to this medicine.

Bao Che Man was a Chinese physician young in years but wise in learning. Using four methods he became so skilled that he found no patients he could not help. The four methods: to look at the patient, to smell him, to speak with him, to know his rhythm in relation with nature's.

With eyes closed and three fingers pressed firmly on a wrist, Dr. Bao received his information. To explain the technique of judging rhythms of nervestream and bloodstream would take a book. After a penetrating diagnosis he would order appropriate herbal preparations usually to be taken as black or brown teas.

One day a woman named Lee Shih came to him. She asked him to make her younger, telling him what he already knew, that the sea-pearl powder would do this for her but that she had no money to buy it.

"I cannot afford to give it to you," he said, "and you cannot buy it. So how shall I help you?"

Lee Shih explained, "When the sea shell opens in its natural environment, sometimes a small bit of sand falls into it, and as it closes it cannot get this irritant out. So it puts a saliva coating around the sand that eventually becomes the pearl. The longer in the making, the larger the pearl."

"We know this," said the physician.

"But what is not known," continued Lee Shih, "Is that the inside of the sea shell, shining as the pearl, is made of the same saliva. How can such a soft creature make such a hard shell? It does, with its sweet sour juices. Its shell made from the same saliva is very cheap, in fact thrown away. If this were known, everyone in China could have such an elixir!"

Dr. Bao looked at her in astonishment. His life intent was to help his people.

"Why does it have such a good effect?" she asked and then answered. "We have two skins, one outside and one within to be cleansed. The powder clinging to our inside skin slowly returns to saliva and antisceptizes the convolutions where food poisons may lodge, so giving us a younger looking skin and delaying our aging. Or our internal rhythms are as sea and shell or pearl."

Dr. Bao made it himself from gathered sea shells, mixing it with suitable herbal remedies into a small pellet in the Chinese manner. He gave it to Lee Shih regularly. A curious effect set in. She seemed to grow both younger and older. "Can it be that my sea-shell powder is only partly as effective as the costly sea pearl?" he asked her.

"Not at all," said Lee Shih. "Do we not see persons making themselves younger and older every day, even momentarily, younger with a mood of joy, older with stiffening concerns and worry? If I may grow both younger and older I am delighted, for then I will stay the same age."

"But I will become older," replied the physician, "and finally you will not have me to give you the potion, and it may not have an equal effect from another."

"True," she replied. "We give not only with our shells but with our heart."

He continued giving her the elixir for one, two, ten years. She kept about the same age, he grew older with a long silvery beard.

"How foolish I was," he thought, "not to have someone give it to me too."

Just then Lee Shih appeared looking as if she had made a discovery. "Let me be your physician," she told him.

"And how shall you treat me?"

"Of course with the sea-shell powder and herbs."

"But I am wondering how much the effect may be in my mind."

"I am mind," Lee Shih answered. "Did I not choose to give me the elixir? Did I not ask and receive your help? Need my mind be apart from that soft and hard, from sea and earth and saliva?"

"You speak as if you were one of our immortals disguised as a lovely women," he commented.

"I am disguised as myself," said Lee Shih, "and so are you. This is why we need medicines. Each thinks itself to be itself or himself or herself."

"Well, isn't it?" asked the doctor.

"It is and it is more, for we are made of the great fullness."

Lee Shih gave him the compound. He too began to seem younger as well as older. He could find nothing in the old books to explain this.

"What is this mind?" he asked Lee Shih one day.

"Ah, that you may not know, good physician," she said, "until you discover it in your heart."

"What do you mean by that?"

"Men die and women age," she explained, "thinking they are men and women. As you put mind or attention *in heart*, both what we call mind and heart dissolve in lightness. Just as the dissolving of the sea shell purifies our blood, so dissolving the mind in heart purifies our human being."

"The ancient philosophy may be true but how do I *do* it?"

"Easily," said Lee Shih. "Touch the top of your mouth with your tongue, sit most easily with eye closed, and *listen in your heart.*"

"What do I listen to?"

"Sounds, tones, words or guidance may or may not come. But thinking and troubling vanish as you *listen*. Believe it or not, our heart's light transforms our worlds."

They live in Hong Kong, which is China, today. Their friends and relatives have aged and passed away. Times have changed but they live on, explaining to no one, for who would believe such a thing possible?

If you go there, become sick, call for a Chinese physician, and happen to get Dr. Bao, you will be lucky indeed.

I take his compound. I do not know what herbs he gives me or what proportion sea shell or pearl. I do not need to know. All I need is to feel his three fingers firmly pressing into my wrists, his eyes closed, his heart listening.

Do not write me for his address. It would be too lonely if you outlived your loved ones unless you could dissolve mind and heart in light. Then, being your own best medicine, you would need no sea-pearl powder.

the world is round
the world is square
and you and I are
everywhere

"Bill!!! I am amazed. We have a POTATO that compels reading. It's so open and easy it traps one into it. POTATO will sell 500 years from now.

Germans found in internment camp, men lived disease free on whole red raw potatos, for five years. A Greenland camp was found, all adults dead, who cooked and ate nothing but potatos. But their children alive who ate peels of same potatos. Reps says: A potato a day keeps the doctor away . . . red . . . raw . . .   reps"

ask
and
it
will
be

POTATO SHOWS HOW TO DO IT

DO NOTHING   NOTHING AT ALL

FOR 5   MINUTES EACH DAY

TO LOOSE EVERY SELF MADE STRESS

OF BODY AND MIND INTRODUCES

THE CONDITION OF TRUE

IMMENSE FRESHING OF DEEP SLEEP

DOUBLE-DOUBLES IN DEEP WAKE

HURRY WORRY TRANSMUTE INTO

WHOLE BE-INGS

LIKE TURNING INSIDE OUT

potato knows how to potato.
each presencing says   HERE HERE
opening uncountable lightpoints.

overlooked fact: no one ever finds a potato, person,
pebbles, place, pause, snowflake the same as itself
or as another.   as it dawns in me in uniquity
that no this and that are the same, then delight I
with and without them as no doubt they are ~~expecting~~
me to delight.   in-viting

6

skying

rooting

beauty award
For having
original Face

reps

Bill—Thanks for note urging me to go functional and give folks things to do. This is what I wish to try in deed and shall try in my own poor way. My subject is

NO NEED TO KILL
11 Ways to Meditate

Now, man, how do you meditate functionally?

and what if everyone is bored and walks out—wouldn't that be fun too?

Dear Bill,

Thanks for your letter, unreporting your journey. Would you believe it, while you were gallavanting with the *houris* I got up at daybreak each morning and improved my book, and often woke up at 12 or 1 and worked 2 hours on it that went like minutes. If 'Centering' had 22 rewritings in Beverly Hills MEDITATE! "WHO, ME?" must have had 32.

When I got it (I thought) done, I sent it to a Dartmouth student and he at once began making copies of it and distributing them. I stopped that.

This showed me I was on a track anyway. I kept at it. What made me answer right away when as a boy my father asked me, "What do you want to be?" I answered, "A writer."

"You can't write!!" he replied.
So I did.
Why?

Why are you you?

Say, man, the MS came back. Why not clean out your closet of 17 other reps MSS too? You sure hoard them. I haven't the faintest idea why. Maybe you're renting them out?

ENTER BREATH

experiment
if you are being breathed
10 breaths a minute
600 an hour 14400 a day
take one play day for your
breath of breath
with heart pause breath pause with single nerve
pulse
eyes closed
or half closed
seeing released
l   e   t breathe
as you let wind blow
rain fall
enter one breath
WHOLLY
going with not against the harmony
"am I already in my breath of life?"
who could be out of it?
we only think us put out
STILL
sit
L E T
breathe
are in themselves deep meditating
before we name them
before we do them
on a day without complaint
*before—ing troubling melts if the human race (you) is
(are) mad (with desires) the act of still sanitizes and
puts you in breath where you belong to live long and
well at home with light and dark.*

INLISTEN

"do we need a teacher?"
we need each one   each presence
each experience teaches us something
more we need response to our
fount of BEing
there is no substitute for inner
guidance our dearest teacher
intuitively within even when without
in our re-act
          in
          silent
          sound
          IS
          the word
          vibrance
          INgendering
          light
          form
          substance
wheat in the field has been found
to grow better with music—sound waves
we grow with silent sound--integrity
do we listen really listen?
to what? to put out meanings?
nationalism, internationalism, racism,
me-ism, as concepts incite us
to purify me is possible
we are doing it most of the time
when we are not doing it
*seeds knows   root knows   sprout knows
          in   silent   sound*

INLIGHT

what we do formally
we freeze
what we do informally
we free
touch finger to forehead
both object-ing and subject-ing
between these
the indescribable experience
          let
          INlight
          turn on
          sit in sun
          or in the light of dark
          seeing released
          in INlight
          consciousness
          be
          light
*"how?" before how pore see wholly see INlight
is instant it reaches through all space we are made of
lightpoints "what is light?" infrontofyouinbackover-
underaroundis this LIGHT*
being alone makes it possible
being alone together
what we ask
into the aroma of a flower
or a stick of incense
may turn us upsidedown
so that all we have falls
out of pockets and
everything is all right
BRIGHT

[Amoeba-like blobs crawl all over the pages of BE! *Reps brushes soft paper with water and then follows with his ink soaked brush. The ink slides over the water, graying it slightly and then dives into dry parts filling them with rich black. The words come later, or not at all.*

We may be a little taken aback by these strange forms, prepared for Reps to ask us, "Do you want to live, to BE? *If your answer is yes then comfortably, oh so comfortably, slightly, slowly, begin an invisible nod 'yes.' You are the way. Don't stop here."]*

PURE WILL

Pure will
is
still.
Will with effort
leaves lines in face.
Try doing something hard
and observe the lines.
Erase them.
Will over another
is resented.
Will with desire
becomes undesirable.
Will for self-gain
brings pain.
Pure will
incredibly penetrative
is still.
Personal will flowers
into impersonal willingness
to re-cognize what we cognize
as gone by, empty,
deliciously
empty.

It is immensely important to distinguish willing from doing and even more important to fuse them.

the First man

BE RELEASED

I have made a remarkable discovery. I can tighten my hands and release them. They compress and let go by my directive and this directive works fast. I also may direct other areas through and even beyond me.
Squeeze hands
tight,
open
bright.

I know that I contract to take a step and release to take the next step. What I did not know was that it is my responsibility to do both. In throwing away my release I throw away my inner life. I have imposed all kinds of binds on this instrument and left them there to ripen into setness, anxiety, bias, opinion. I propose that such self-impositions be released. "How?" Be released!

Sit in an easy balancing position. Firmly gently direct, "Release, all stress, in head." Let it. Let it in its own good way and time. It will. Do not wait for it to do so but proceed with the next directive. "Release, all stress, in face." Continue giving such directives slowly surely through

head
face
nostrils
eyes
ears
cheeks
lips
mouth
neck
back
backbone
middle
shoulders
arms
hands
body base
legs
feet . . . .

At first you may choose to have a friend give you the directives and to do them with you. Like letting sunlight into a closed room, it brings wondrous refreshment. It may accomplish in minutes what still sitting without it may after years.
"Then what do I do?"
First, BE RELEASED.
Then BE RELEASED *lying down, sitting, standing, moving.*
Be YOU.

Forgotten man

PRIMALLY

We have the finest known instrument loaned us, our human one. How shall we use it? Presently in an iron age of much misuse of nature and human nature, we are catching glimpses of the golden age to come. You may be in it now.

Have you a mind? Our mind or spirit, invisible, untouchable, instantly in one place then another, unborn, undying, uses matter as its instrument.

We speak of mind or spirit but the reality far exceeds our words about it. Each feels "I am" unitively, wholly, affirming BEing. We recognize BEing in animal and young child. Neither has learned an alphabet yet both know well the alphabet of BEing.

We take our primal experiencing for granted. Hunger is primal. So are waking, sleep, moving. Giving our life for another is primal. Birds live primally. Seeing is primal, We see through eyes. We see. "Who is this one who sees?" The one insaying me in each one.

On the side of a mountain in Hawaii while typewriting these words I hear someone along the road typewriting too, then to the left, then to right. A bird is singing the sound of the typewriter keys.

"Bill—Yes you are right/ the esoteric scene is passing as fashions always are. But it is also swelling so appearing not to pass. But changing. Glad you like SIT IN. *I thot the Zen Center did a fine job of it. I had nothing to do with format. Why not excerpt from* SIT IN *using any of the pictures you want with the text sort of writ all over. One full page.*

reps "

[*The entire text of* SIT IN *appears below.*]

SIT IN

Head and heart are not apart.

Sit in in-vites you into new experience as new all through doing (no thing) well. In the Orient those who sit in become stronger healthier and surer of their cosmos position. So may you. Humans from over the world visit these sitters and often wonder what they are doing. This book explains what so they may visit you.

The act of sit in takes self discipline. Then it takes self guidance. Even to take a step you guide it. Then it takes other guidance: the coming together of cosmos as you, accepting this togethering thankfully, graduating from dissatisfaction. All this packs *in* sit. Keep in, before words about it. Do not go beyond in. As men give their life for country give yours for life itself. In any position or act of good will graduate in. Please compose ourself. This may take a little while, then . . .

As you sit in, without moving even a finger, with a friend present or present elsewhere.
1 minute the first day.
2 minutes the second day.
3 minutes the third day.
Increasing minutely up to 10.
Or later maybe more.

Preferably at the same time place perhaps in an empty quiet room. Your integrity begins to show. Cell rhythms smooth in and you feel better and better.

When standing we balance our human instrument as three inverted triangles:

Head into shoulders
Shoulders into pelvis
Pelvis into feet.

As this mobile balancing leans slightly muscle stress begins to recover us into weightless. Perfect. Bliss this.

As we compose our lowest triangle into a firm base including our whole body In-ing begins. Sitting crosslegged on a hard cushion or forward on a low flat seat with both feet on ground something amazing happens.

We	*open*
Shut	*up*
Up	*in*

Sit comfortably then most comfortably erect, centering your weight equally on two sit bones. Forehead smooth, soft eyes near closing, inbreathflow high through nostrils. Shoulders releasing, back firm, neck soft, jaw not tight. Head floating up from back as if about to nod yes,

though not yet nodding. The sitting itself your answer. The sitting itself your healing. Just do it. Difficult when stiff. More and more fluidly flexive when firm and gentle with you.

Impulse subdued.
Emotive re-act pacified.
Radiance through.

Too simple to believe in experiencing. Millions of years before yoga, thousands of years before zen, re-discovered gloriously by buddha (2500 years ago) and other sages and variously formalised. If a dull moment comes, stretch loosen *in*.

ZEN KISS

"What is it like?"
Like inlight. Actually we are made of light, too instant for birth death.
"How?"

Observe natural breathflow
Outbreathflow.
Inbreathflow.
Imagine turning palms of hand
Down with outbreathflow
'Up with inbreathflow.
Continuing without moving hands
In our rhythm of suns and seas
Given with birth.
Lo...the great harmony

"Are you dreaming it?" Waking from dream and from waking dream graduate *in*. "Does it help others?" Are you others? Are others you? Is empty full? "Can it be done with overstepping, overdoing, overgoing?" Yes. "Does it get to be a habit?" If you sit and sag, try too hard, try to repeat it.

It's electric.
Just as it sits.

Earned benefits of *sit in* may be due in part to:

a) Your willing to practice it as an act of integrity.
b) Charging your batteries, minding your business.
c) doing nothing beyond *in*.
d) Mind attention accommodating one aggregate at a time wholly.
e) Smoothing broken breathflow.
f) In-viting innate nerveflow, bloodflow, lymphflow, juiceflow, cell consciousnessing.
g) Pressures on large base, nerve cluster, opening inner doors to tophead.
h) Entering silent sound. Awarefullness.
i) Self-learning to do (no-thing) when about your daily work. Moving water-smooth, light-bright, so nothing is the water.
j) Multiple other reasons unknown as yet to us air and light breathers.

Is. In this lifetime *is* resolves to help one individual . . . you . . . so wondrously put together. Who me?

Something is immediate, unchanging in change, inchanting me me in each grassblade. "Who me?" Instead of me or I, may one answer.

IS--is does it.
Is sits.
Fresh! shouts the bud.

Strengthening, trueing, utterly still. You may feel it is meditating or praying or composing or graduating from talk-back.
Before before say
Keep in
Firm as pyramid
In deep wake
As in deep sleep
Instantly regenerating
Rejuvenating.
New life begins here.
Thank you for your life.

Our energy sea sees us. Earth and its creatures are negative to light. We break through to inlight.

"This book gives some things to let do, already doing—to have you new all through.

Why do a book cultivating me when nuclear war, lack of fresh air, starvation, disease, unease, fake food are falling on us fast? Agreed. We face a life/death reality. How to face it subjects this work. It proposes a new orienting—not kill but let; not apart but including other life forms with ours; not out-think but feel.

We need a new human on earth. Could this new human be you?"

[From the preface to JUICING]

JUICING

Let eyes close, let lips touch. Taste, feel juices transforming. We are 80% fluidic, 90% light, 100% us. Would you like to feel good all through? Sweeten your juices:

                nerveflowjuice
                bloodflowjuice
                lymphflowjuice
                vitalflowjuice

You have the power to sweeten or sour your juiceflow at once.

Lavish statement: Our body has one trillion (1,000 billion) cells each one wiser than we are each immersed in all-conscious protoplasm. Another way to be good to your juiceflow: Stop complaining.

Start thanking.

SOFTENING

"Where do I hear music?" In me. "Where do I feel pain?" In me. You cannot touch or taste for me—but I can. You cannot see or hear for me—but I can. During my lifetime so far I have known magnificent exemplars but they were helpless to learn for me.

Indulgence weakens, INTEGRITY strengthens seeing. I see a mountain, I see myself climbing it. If I INsee myself not climbing I'm not going to make it. We name this faith and doubt. May we actually INsee and INhear distant events? Indians of the upper Amazon can. Yogins of India have done so for centuries. A mother somehow INsees her distant child. One sense interweaves with another although our sensings are mostly out of use.

May we graduate through sensing? After total release of seeing, looking from where *seeing* looks, what do we see?

"SEEING"

Right, yet as I say "I see it" and overlook *seeing* I tangle in "I" and "it" and am hooked as a fish out of water. Fish *in* water is the *seeing*.

INLIGHTING

We touch a button to light a room. What button may we touch to INlight us? May we turn from seeing out to INsight??

Hold arm out and point to something, then curve fingers in to palm. How do you do this? Considering honestly we must answer, "I don't know." In this "don't know" instantly experience your potential true whereof all this springs. By all means let us be this honest with ourself.

STRETCHING

Flexive = young, stiff = old. You choose. Youth the world over makes some slight low-powered adjustment to feel good. Whatever troubles, let it through without reacting to it. Whatever pleases, let it through without reacting to it.

Nothing is the matter.

SLEEP

being   BEING
BEING   being
    In deep sleep
    hybernation
    one life
sapping

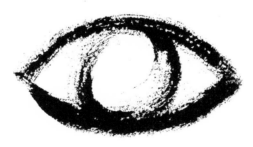

WAKING

You know how you fall asleep each night. Why not fall awake?

Fact: No one sees. We are shown "it", "it", in INlight so fast it seems motionless, true as you.

Are you reading these words? What are you doing to them? What are they doing to you? Are they tightening you? Or loosening you as a gentle breeze across your cheek?

Each one is best, best, best? Unique in uniquity, each offers something rare. No two pebbles leaves snowflakes time places faces the same.

PAUSING

"Why pause?" Why go out of breath?
Breath paused,
heart paused,
heart paused,
life paused,
into the next moment life.

We pause between words said in slow step; seeing, hearing, replying as bliss this.

To brighten eyesight fill mouth with water and splash water over eyes. Empty mouth. Lower head slowly. Wait, witness beauty of leaf, pause, harmony of sound.
tip of nose . . . fragrance
tip of tongue . . . flavor
middle of tongue . . . touch
root of tongue . . . sound
flex toes, touch fingertips, joints juicing, who shall you thank for such gifts?

STANDING

Head floating up from back, eyesoft, jawloose, soft-kneed, inlightly, heels touching, as if about to go three ways at once. Let weight forward into balls of feet and, without stepping, swing both heels out so feet are parallel for integrity and apart for stability.
Strong.
Tireless.
Primitive.

SQUEEZE

Squeeze hands tight, open bright. Squeeze all through.
Releasing face while opening hands
Releasing shoulders while opening hands
Releasing body base while opening hands

Constrictions dissolve, congestions vanish. Nothing could be more important. Don't do it for any reason. If you do something for some reason you are put out. Be found IN whatever "it" is.

MOVING

Smooth Motion Cures Commotion
smooth: even, steady, unbreaking
motion: a melting of one position into another
cures: relieves
commotion: fear, suffering

Whenever you feel uncomfortable what do you do? You move. Whenever you feel joyfull you move. Be faster than think. Think faster than feel. Feel faster than do. Why then move slow? Not fast, not slow, invisibly evenly, as old garments falling away, nakedly innocently. Is this how new humans are born?

skin
of onion
thinking

LET

Let breathflow as you do—in your rhythm of suns and seas, given with your conception. As water flows in great harmony. This is all we need to do—to be breathed—with outbreathflow equal to inbreathflow.

Few accomplish this even once in a lifetime.

NOW

Where is Buddha? Where is Jesus? Where are you?

Each forest tree rests in *unchange.* timeless spaceless IS.(The dream procession of change would pull us out of ME.)

The easiest thing to do seems to us the hardest: to let all self-imposed pressures off our nerve blood networks. *To sit and look, to sit and listen, then to move* interests us. Even more interesting may be to sit in one's given breathflow and let go with it—friend of birds and clouds.

STEMMING

Tree, receiving untold news through these roots, delight through leaves, windblown flexively, beyond suffering, beyond bliss, this.

With deep respect for (great nature) Japanese farmers bow before small wood shrines in the ricefields (silently thanking).

To overflow do nothing at all. If you do something you only use up energy, self-filling as you let it (as in deep sleep) As energy overflows feel good. How simple, how profound. Let it. Do nothing while doing something.

SIT

It's raining dewing sprinkling showers of golden light so fine so pure wherever you sit
S
T
I
L
L

EAT

To breathe LIGHT, open nostrils. To end starvation on earth, eat air. Close eyes when chewing. Share.

Can you fast from food? You do so each night. Can you fast from possessing? You learn to. Can you fast from breathflow? In breathflow pause. Can you fast from death? Born, as we are, each moment.
Drinking water, water drinks me.
Breathing air, air breathes me.
Experiencing LIGHT, INlights me.

SHARING

You must act, your breathflow compels it. You speak on outbreathflow, exert on outbreathflow. You must receive, your inbreathflow invites it. Giving and receiving the day night of life. One without the other misses the point.

The Beneficence. Do you have feet and toes? Do you have hands and fingers? Do you have eyes? Are you in a position? Do you move? Can you tell what a bird flying does for us? Can you sense what the aroma of a flower does for us? If the answer is YES to one of these questions, you are in the *beneficence.*

INSINGING

We communicate with words, commune with *silencing.* To hide the tribe's position Amerindian mother holds the child's mouth shut. Mother—hold mine.

WHOLLY

Eagle sees better, deer hears better, bear smells better, cat moves better than we do. But we drive a car and talk better and better. We look into countless objects trying to find the object and pull apart objects trying to find the subject.

My instrument needs some oil of lovingkindness. If I cannot sit at once into utmost bliss . . .
Rest assured
Head and heart   not apart

We   yawn—ah   exclaim—oh
we—eeee   coo—uuuu   Silent
sound,   noh sound, we are.   Sub-silent
sound:
eeeeeeeeeeeeee
                      electric
aaaaaaahhhhhhh
                    energizing
ooooooooooohhhh
                    enfolding
uuuuuuuuuuuuuu
                    revealing

bud
adoring
sun

[*Every day Reps get up and writes a book. At least it seems that way to the editors, publishers and friends who are fortunate enough to be on the receiving end of his inspirations. Since he writes these books faster than publishers can publish them, the world may never see books entitled* SIPPING WITH A WOODEN SPOON, NON-BOOK, GOO GURU, *and* SECRET TEACHINGS OF PAUL REPS.

Lately Reps has been experimenting with collections of 8-8 page Reps books, 1 book to a large folded sheet of paper, slipped into a simple box. And his friends have been transcribing and editing Reps' talks for eventual publication. Meanwhile we present selections from some of his current unpublished works below. IN THE LAND OF ZO, *another recent unpublished work, appears at the beginning of this chapter.*]

from MANUAL FOR LIVING

RADIATE

No one believes in angels
Everyone believes in angels (secretly)

We package light. When busy we are busy lighting up. Our INvisible lightness shapes our form as a hand shapes a glove. It does so through electromagnetic groupings of innumerable light-points. These lightpoints pervade us. Above them other configuration swirls have been named angels by humans of many races. These "angels" always act for our protection and guidance.

My angel is more helpful to me than I am. Usually I am not aware it even exists though any child will tell me it does. Babies talk with their angels.

"So what do you suggest?"

Phone or write your angel: *Dear Angel--let me thank you and thank you for guiding me so well. May you continue to do so and may I deserve it.*

Whether you name it a spirit of guidance or a center of intuition or an angel or soul does not matter. What matters is that you have an invisible friend and helper. You are not alone in this world or another.

Whether angels are pre-born or post-born or electric whorls does not matter. What matters is that you never are without one who does everything possible and impossible to help you grow in love and harmony pulsing through universe.

Call on your angel or on angels of others when you need help. Receive it lightly.

Be your own angel.

Saints and sages in India have made themselves so receptive that they could not be moved. One of them used to ride around Dahl Lake in Kashmir on a large flat stone. The stone is still there. Miracles are done with intense in-picturing. Take a look at something troubling you. Change the look, imaging it as perfect. We need the wisdom of a seed.

If you journey to old India and study Yoga with a sincere teacher (who never charges), then ask, "What is the core of it all?" your answer may well be, "Have head lower than heart."

Respect for sky and earth amplifies your worth. Bowing, bowing head to ground, lying head down on a hill or on a slanted board, crawling, lowering eyes then head, facilitates bathing brain with blood.

Sit before a table. Pound on table with both fists declaring "I'm growing younger, I'm growing younger, I'm growing younger." Continue. The rhythmic pounding has you ambidextrous, increasing overall circulation. Your declaring begins coming true if you mean it. It is easy to make or break a habit this way. Find it 100 times more effective than a pill.

from SUCK

INVITATION

I invite you to touch the button on the wall. As you do the l i g h t goes on. I in-vite you to touch the button in you. As you do (y)our in-light flashes on. Where then in you is this button? Your belly button? Your sex button? Your heart core? The l i g h t within (y)our forehead? YES YES YES YES all of these places and when you jump for JOY and when you slightly smile and as you feel YES or NO and mean it.

We are made of l i g h t points, trillions of them packaging us, suns of suns condensing into us. You may call them pores or energy or ki or chi or prana or presence but experience them wholly as you blink. Image-imagine your very l i g h t n e s s and be as you ARE centering universe deliciously. Too fast for words, before lightning strikes, prethink, pre-me, pre.

Play it. Until fun better left undone.

HOW TO GROW YOUNGER INSTEAD OF OLDER

To grow younger instead of older flood the brain with blood for a while each day. As you upsidedown or as you bend over in a deep sustained bow or as you rest on the floor with feet up on bed the flooding begins curing you of worry hurry.

Soon you stop complaining, fearing, trembling heartflow. You appreciate quality instead of quantity. You just feel fresh. Best of all you stop jabbering, in and out of mouth.

HOW TO BE YOU

You already ARE, so need do nothing at all.

"Asleep? Awake?" Surely you are you in deep sleep and in deep waking, even when storms blow through your life.

"More specifically?" *BLINK* in center of head. Let breathflow flow from center of heart lightheartedly. We are made of l i g h t. Uncountable energy points flash us. This way scientists 'see' electrons and atoms. As we move, take a step, lift a finger, we move as l i g h t, just as we are and shall always be in some form or other.

As attention turns inward outer concerns lighten, lessen. In this direction humans pray, meditate, celebrate, study, play games, just look.

SEE AND SAY

Looking into
    another's eyes
coming   closer until
    eyes become one

from HOW TO FEEL REAL GOOD

PLAYABLE

Each year for six I study with the consummate movement teacher of China who also heals, never charges, never oversteps, never loses touch. A bone in my foot goes out of place. I happen to meet him in an elevator.

"How do I put a bone in my foot in place?"

"Shake it," he replies as he leaves the elevator.

I blink at the sharp answer. I shake the foot. It works. Now I shake away constriction, cramp, pain, anything.

Stand, shake fingers, hands, arms so loose even feet shake. Try shaking yourself seriously.

MOVABLE

We are like the telephone company with us as president of countless employees and miles of wire and wireless. If we give an order "I feel bad" they have us feeling bad and if we declare "just a little better" somehow we feel better. When we give confusing orders they sit there chewing gum.

Point to something, now point strongly through it. Feel the difference? Let there be pointing and a friend to pull down your arm as you point. Arm pulls down easily.

Now extend ENERGYFLOW through and beyond your arm 100 miles as you point. Your arm will be most difficult to pull down.

"What does it mean?" It means ENERGY-FLOW manifests as you will it. Point strongly with a silent "BE WELL" to someone not well. They begin to feel better. A cut heals more quickly as you blow on it and feel it healing as you blow.

Subatomic transforming is possible with full attention. Tibetan yogins experiencing heat from a flame in heart sit on a block of ice and melt it in subzero weather.

Stand and point straight down with every atom including arms and hands. You will be very heavy to lift.

PRESENCE

Have 6 photos taken of your face, one after the other. Each will be different. Place 12 rocks around a larger one in a sand circle. By moving one rock or by walking around them or by blinking the relations change.

DO NOTHING
WHILE DOING NOTHING

Under your *go go* and *do do* find a most surprising way. With enormous thanks to body and total still of mind--DO NO THING. Will you let do it? How long does it take to put you together in your perfect be-ing? However long, it comes to now.

perhaps only
        perhaps
you stand beside me
  in the gentle rain

Buddha compassion
Jesus Love
and touch of a hand

cut some humans from their stems
tie them in a bunch
Pull a Few out
Stick them in a vase
Look at them

throw
the
rest
away

Human arrangement
by Flowers

Little bud
open this heart
with your
invisible hands

reps assured

[*On every subject from sex to death
including ways to live, to breathe,
to eat, to travel, to play*]

we wake as angels
and go to sleep as devils

because we don't know how
to spend our waking day

let me tell you how!

"dear neck,
Let go"

REPS ASSURED:

This chapter could well be called "Health and Travel," but it is much more than that. Since he first went to India before World War I, Paul Reps has been exploring.

He was carrying around a bag of sprouts twenty years ago. He saw and wrote of the danger of polluted air and water when "ecology" was a word known only to scientists. Over the last twenty years (the time span of the letters which follow) he has delighted in the clean air of the Norwegian fjords, roamed the desert from Agadir to Marrakesh, been an honored guest at dinners in Hong Kong, and built his own home on a small Hawaiin island.

One theme which runs through almost every letter to Bill is: what, where, and how we could live, eat, travel, heal, breathe. In 1963 he was experimenting with Macrobiotics; in 1968 he was jogging with one of the greatest athletic trainers in the world on the soft spring moss in Sweden, and he was visiting the Phillipines to see the "miracle healers" at work. For many years he practised T'ai-Chi with a great Chinese master and, wherever he goes, he exemplifies his own words: "Smooth motion cures commotion." Throughout his life he has experimented with and written about healthful ways to move and breathe, when the practitioners of these methods were still little-known and difficult to find.

In the letters which follow, Reps shares with Bill his delights and discoveries on every subject from sex to death. He gives Bill suggestions on how best to heal himself from serious accidents in 1962 and 1971. He encourages him again and again to try to leave New York City for the sake of his sanity or, if he must stay, how to in-joy more, how to "play it."

Though the letters are not arranged chronologically, we have noted the years the letters were written for those curious as to what Reps was discovering where and when. When we were editing this book we asked Reps how he felt about our including all this material. We pointed out that some of these practices have since been discredited. "That's all right," he told us, "Everything gets discredited eventually." Rest assured.

ON SEX:

Interviewer: I want to ask you about sex. Now, there are some religious groups who feel that to abstain from sex is the best way to grow spiritually or just to grow. And I'm sure that in your travels you've come across people who have had that as part of their world view. What do you think about that, to abstain or not to abstain in terms of growth?

Reps: Oh, I don't like your word "spiritual" because I wonder if you are just reiterating it, saying it, using it as a concept. But the word "spiritual" could be, I feel, "inspirited". I feel very spirited, but not spiritual. That's my reaction to that particular overused word. I don't think there's any difference between spirit and matter and I think that word says that this is spiritual but that doesn't matter so much or that is matter, so I don't think the use of the word "spiritual" as separated from material is quite proper. Now what was your question?"

Interviewer: Question was—to feel spirited, that some groups may feel that to abstain from sex, physical sex is . . .

Reps: Oh yeah, about sex. Everybody has a special view on sex and they're welcome to it. So I have no special view because I'm not trying to steer people around. If they're going to do nothing but complain, why I
think that's wonderful,
that's what they want to live by.
If they're going to go into a lot
of sex or no sex, I think that's
wonderful because that's what
they're going to learn to live with.
So I have no dogma about
eating and no dogma about sex.
I think each person expresses their
vital life by themselves.
But I only have the
dogma of don't lie
and don't steal
and don't borrow money.

[From an interview with Reps
in Boulder, Colorado 6/22/79]

My Four Wives

... importuned to take a wife during his sojourn in Japan, Reps answered with the poem, Four Wives, published by the musician Nakajima.

All summer my lovely wife complained.
When I asked her why, she said it was too hot.

When I asked my winter wife why she scolded so,
she said it was too cold.

    This was why I deserted them
      for a Spring wife and for a wife of Fall.

At first this worked well
my Spring wife dancing and gay,
my wife in Fall in beauteous robes
and her embraces as feathers of silk.

But each summer time my Spring wife disappeared
and in the winter my wife of Fall was nowhere to be found.
Thus summer and winter was I lonely
and spring and autumn, glad,
and I was but half alive,
living without a wife for half each year.

    Yet there was nothing to be done
      for when a man chooses wives
      he must endure his choices.

Nor could I find anyone who could tell me what to do
until one day wandering in a woodland
I came upon a hut with a sign over the door marked Sage.
Surely this sage will tell me, I thought.
So I asked him.

[From Gentry, Spring 1955]

So h e told me: Make a meeting of your four wives and ask them.
I wrote them letters they never answered.
This angered me so I went back and burned down the sage's hut.
Out of the ashes I brewed a tea.
It had a sourish taste and as I drank it
I grew suddenly both hot and cold.
Sparks danced in my eyes and I could see
flowers growing quickly into buds.
Brilliant leaves fluttered from the ground
up upon the trees again.

How can I be hot and cold together, I wondered,
and how can flowers become buds and leaves turn green again?
I felt as if all my wives were singing with me
and there was nothing to be gained or lost
and no seasons nor birth nor death
nor desire nor fear nor any pain or pleasure.

It is like this in the center of sun, the sage seemed
to be explaining,
for from here your wives have issued forth
and from here day and night begin and everything human and natural.

Enveloped in a great white light
I was much more than the I with four wives.
Now all women were my wives and all men as myself
and this myself a great mystery.

Sculptures by PAUL REPS
Photos by MILTON ALTMAN

If it had not been for my wives
I might never have met the sage
and if I had not met the sage
I would never have burned down his hut
and made tea and entered sun
and known all beings as one.

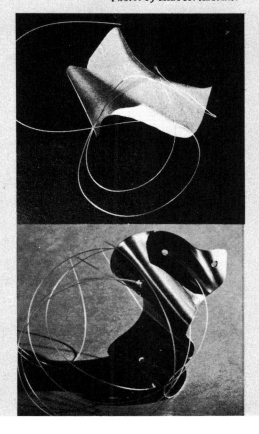

Does this seem dreamlike or strange to you?
Is life out of water strange to the fish?
Is flying in air strange to the worm?
of course.
Yet beings live out of water
and fly above earth
and some men have four wives and even more.
And though they may not know it yet
humans see and feel and move
as light.

Walking far in the mts today
in the bright sun after the
typhoon yesterday I came to
an Inn named Tokuzawa and
sat on a wood bench a yard
from one end of it. A girl
was washing her face and
arms in the stream. When
she finished she came and
sat beside me, putting her
knapsack down, she did this
so innocently + so friendly. She
had left Tokyo at 10 P.M, rode the train until central
4 A.M.
At Matsumoto she took an electric train
to Shima Shima and a bus for
3 Hrs to Kamikochi; the world is round
then hiked 4 the world is square
to where she and you and I are
through the mts everywhere 5 miles
to return met me on her way alone
2 days. I always to Tokyo in
and listen to watch people's movements
tell about them. So as she left I shook her
hand. It was like warm putty in
mine, accommodating wholly. I never
felt such a handshake.   over

Can this be how lines were first
formed in hands? (innocently)
Japanese girls, and I meet so many
know this accomodation
instinctively. It is part of their
happiness. It comes from the
farmer wife according with
the judgment of her man who
decides when & what to plant to
survive. One boss, many
accordants. 5 or 10 years ago
no girl would be hiking alone
or speak to a foreigner. The times
have freed the woman, or given
her an independent experience.
Everyone carries a camera and along
with her load she had one.
I explained we are given uncounted
pictures each day we may let
appear through us so we need not
possess them. This may be a
next step to free. By the way
she was quite lovely and
sumptuously dressed. I have
no children in Japan.

this year
1 month Boulder, colo. 5000 ft
1   "   Valadolens...   2000 "
1   "   Kamikochi   5000 "
1   "   Norway 2-3000
                       12,000.

YOU GAVE ME HIS $10,000.00 (TEN THOUSAND DOLLAR) BOOK.

Dear Bill,

Ohsawa talked twice yesterday, superbly. He told
about may cures of diseases by persons using his methods.
He probably is the greatest doctor in the world. He is humble
modest, quiet, considerate, strong, black haired and most
vigorous at 70. He leaves for Japan Sep 7th.

SUGAR in any form turns out to be the sancerous
thing. Glucose is made by starch, brown rice, in mouth and
sugar manifactured fights this, takes 3 months to get out of
system.

SLOW EATING and UNDEREATING are dures and overeating
the best food is worst. Kevran proves the transmutation of
elements in the human body, and it happens when we do not eat also.

OVERSWELLING by too much liquid ingestion
makes a cure or health impossible.

YANG AND YIN foods and how they affect us
is important. Perhaps the most dramatic sudden cures spring
from stopping sugar, poisons as medicines and vitamins,
overdrink, etc. and eating brown rice. This is a complete
reversal say in a week. Less dramatic is the steady
remaking of tissues through daily observation of his approach.

Dr Norita with him is completely free ,he says.
This Dr cured 600 incurables in Japan, instructed his wife
to continue and is travelling around the world, freely.
Hurrah.

Drs in South America are getting big results
with the method. Also in Europe. I have written an article
about Ohsawa.

reps

Aug 18, 63
Box 238, Chico, Calif.

[*Reps wrote an article on Ohsawa which appeared, in different forms, in* The Mainichi (*a Tokyo newspaper*), *in* Bill's magazine American Fabrics and Fashions *and later in Reps' book* SQUARE SUN SQUARE MOON. *At the time Reps wrote the letter below, he and Bill were discussing the possibility of publishing a brochure detailing Ohsawa's teaching.*]

Dear Bill,   [*1963*]

Here is the original *Mainichi* article and additional pages necessary to make a suitable brochure of the whole thing. If you do this please use the text exactly as in *Mainichi* article. The breakup of the article is brighter in *AF*, but the subject is a life or death one and I think should not be illustrated at all; — that is, Reps should not inject his drawings with it. The title is so terrific that it carries itself.

Mainichi got many responses, everyone likes the article and it is indeed the first time in the 40 year life of Ohsawa for Macrobiotics that he has had a clear statement of it.

The reason for this may be that doctors are notoriously poor at writing or communicating. However when Ohsawa gets into communication *with an individual* he runs in high gear. He is a 1 to 1 person.

I think you are a terrific 1 to 1 person also but that
    a) you don't know this or
    b) use it as consciously as you might.

Bill, it is almost impossible to get a hotel in either Tokyo or Kyoto and they want to put you out at the exact termination of your reservation. It looks like all over the world people have discovered Japan, including the Japanese who anyway are great travellers internally. I travel internally when I eat buckwheat groats and brown rice. Ohsawa likes the buckwheat even better than the rice. I eat with him in Tokyo, and have lived with his successor in Osaka.

As you know I poem it, and do not write sequentially. But in the *Mainichi* article it is all a flowing sequence. You have rearranged it better in your *AF* article and for your magazine it looks better and probably needs to be treated more lightly.

But how can I tell you how to set up a page of *AF*? I can't. Just exuberate it. I felt when you rearranged the article it lost power. Even if it needed it, even if poorly paragraphed, an anyone should be allowed to speak his piece. Then it comes through.

If you try to come through with two or more, constructing comes in and inspiring fades out. Jesus said in Heaven (where we should be) there is no marrying or giving in marriage; Reps he says, "There is no marriage among the grassblades." But how does he know? Maybe one can possess another. I give you   you.

Against this view it takes a dozen guys to make a page. But someone pastes the fabric swatches on in joy. It's the joy that makes the page. The priceless ingredient.

There is *a deep flow* of purpose in the writing from *Mainichi* and the added pages herewith and if you are going to do a brochure at all it should be with this flow, not with a rearranging. I am, in short, shaking the world with the thing.

Already I have a man who wishes to translate it into European languages. Ohsawa has centers over the world who will want it as it is the only thing they have to give to a person who then can decide at once, YES or NO. Moreover the drugs and medicines and living manner are increasing sickness at such a rate that the demand is just beginning.

BILL!

We have had weeks of sun weather perfect
with a very few rains mostly nights.
Always surprising weather.

The Greek and the Japanese idea that
eating only rice is healing
is because rice sweeps thru and absorbs
poisons as it nourishes, (protein poisons)
so brown rice only should be our perfect food.

But **HUNGER**
is still better.
Many of us never know **HUNGER** in our
lifetime, only appetite.

I am now cultivating

HUNGER

thanks to Cora
thanks to Bill
thanks to
thanks to chrow
thanks to Ohsawa
thanks to rice
thanks to

one seed
buds
10,000 seeds

Dear Marielle,   [*1979*]

I HAVE TAKEN ONE PELLET OF KH3!

I have two months supply, 60, come from Ireland. Thanks to YOU. How much shall I send for them? Where?

If I begin growing younger tissuewise in a month or two do I grow old without them? Why shouldn't KH3 make me younger?! As I do according to my faith it comes about! What price, faith?

Hindus use ashes for such purposes, blessed by the gooroo's hands or hand if not ambidextrous. Surely KH3 is as good as ash. How much does it cost and how can I get it?

K means a picture of *LIGHTNING* unexpected
H stands for organized or disorganized
3 means child, expression

Dear Marielle,

I had sent me a book REJUVENATION SECRETS FROM AROUND THE WORLD by Paavo Airola and in it I first read about KH3. As we read there, to give it a fair trial we should take it 3 to 5 months then a month break then a repeat.

But I only have 60 capsules from you, a 2 month supply. I believe in it, from your strange observation that your friend went to school with your father yet is now young!

I myself am feeling very good but I take special care of myself too and eat minimally which I find helps.

Also, look here, you are a woman. Woman all like to be young. How about you taking it? Maybe you are. Bill cannot take it as his subconscious has been indoctrinated with doubt. It takes a simpleton like me to take a chance. I am an unreasonable person.

Rest assured,

Bill —   [1971]

I have heard Soen-san is dying in Japan,
so have written him a method to save his life,
you leave on Tuesday for Paris
any word?

AIRMAIL LETTER TO A ZEN TEACHER
    ABOUT TO LEAVE THIS WORLD.

Dear Roshi-san—
Must you leave us?
Do this.
Have a healthful friend
press your form with thumbs
from head to feet,
pressing slowly in rhythm
with natural breath.

Press *GOOD* with natural
outbreathflow
and
FEEL ENERGY-INTAKE FROM
WHOLE COSMOS THROUGH BONES
with inbreathflow —

Continue —

He lives!

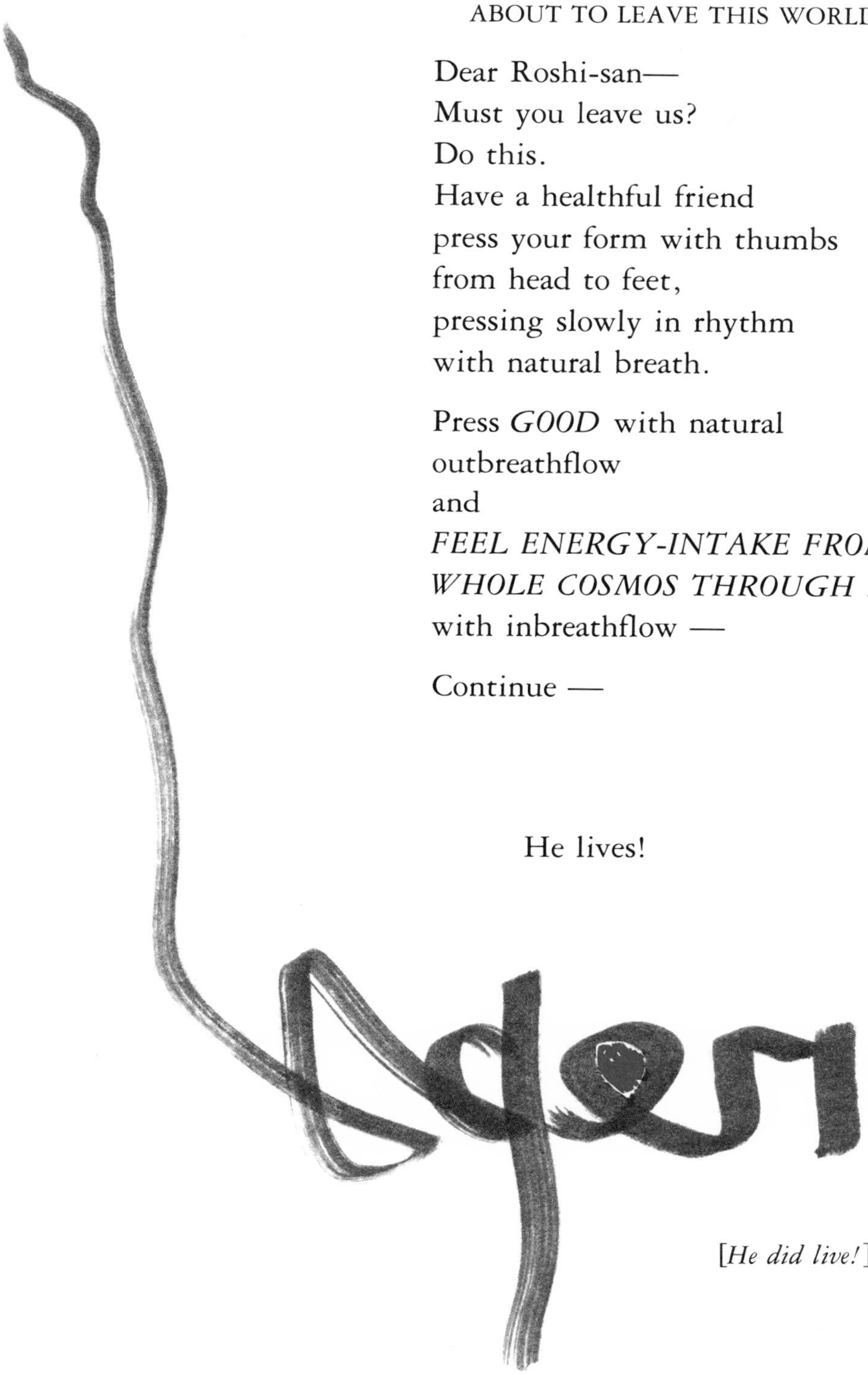

[He did live!]

Bill,   [*1973*]

   When you get this I will have fasted 14 days and *never* got hungry due to 2 hour program of fruit juices etc. I have lost 10 lbs. excess and *learned how to eat* and have mastered my nibbling food lust, neural excitement, and my whole life is changed for the better.

   I did this with 150 other fasters; swam, hiked, tripped with no weakness except a dullness for the first 2 or 3 days when my years of poisons were ejecting. It is a compulsory rest and calming, surely out of this world. So I recommend it for you and Marielle as a way to live longer better if you have the guts to self-search.

Bill,   [*1978*]

   I was received by Ramamurti Yogi who embraced me, put my hands on his head for my blessing and ordered his followers to bow down to me as a buddha.

   That's not the point.

   The point is was that he had repeated strokes but did not die.

   In disgust he gave up all food theories and went on 2 cups of honey a day and milk diet.

   It cleaned him out so he was living in total *BLISS*.

Maybe we need cleaning out?

SAVE YOUR LIFE   [*1964*]

It is easy to stop smoking.
You simply yell at your mind,
"STOP!"
It gets scared.
You never want to smoke again.
But you must mean it.

                              reps

Dear Bill,   [*1974*]

Once in 1930, bottom of depression, my innocent faithful mother said, "Things will be all right."
She called the bottom with her faith.

The other day she came to me and said the same thing.

Do you think we can commune with the dead or wish the living dead? I consider all people living as
dead, practically speaking.

Dear Bill,   [*1975*]

The young man who told me about the miracle of moshe feldenkrais, straightening out by
muscle moving a severely crippled woman in an hour, also tells me he has two books published, the
first one too thinky, and that he will be part of the time in NYC.

Should you wish to pursue this, a treatment by him might possibly be beneficial to you and
hardly could hurt anything so I report this to you.

BILL!!   [*1968*]

Do you know of the miracle workers of phillipines? There have been two.

Having heard so much good from so many Japanese here I accompanied 4 of them to this healer
AND HAD 16 OPERATIONS in two sessions.

He can open heart and brain and other parts of body with bare hands, he does so and all bad
things clots etc. issue out of body as mine did   a very bloody affair   no pain whatever.

It is a bloody thing takes 15 minutes a session only but he may be the greatest man in world. 5 of
us were together in our sessions, all benefitted.

He says I will live way beyond 93-94 due to this cleansing. He removed two growths from brains
of two women in our party. One looked at once no longer as if she were dying but like a happy little
girl. The other could not even touch her hair it was so painful before; she could easily at once after the
growth had been removed from her head, half as large as little finger etc. etc.

I will not write of this nor assume responsibility of giving details to others except in person. He
has been doing this 30 years. Stick around, kiddo, we may learn something.

HOW TO LEVITATE

The intention of these directions: To completely ease our thousands
of fine nerve-muscles in the skin and cranial cages, that we and
those around us may be lighter, enlightened.

(1) Lie face down on a firm surface. Let your attention, your
consciousness, get heavier and heavier through every cell on
outbreaths—until you feel you are sinking into the earth and on
into the center of the earth.

(2) Since it is quite warm here at the center, you will finally stop
sinking and float. This begins levitation. (1) and (2) cannot hurt
you in any way and are much easier than digging a hole and
climbing down into earth. Do not be afraid to float in your cells.

(3) Now continue this delicious rest or floating in a standing
position. With practice you may float even when upright.

(4) Continue this feeling as you move gently forward and
back a step.

(5)You are now directing both vertical and horizontal lines through
the organism. Form is the awareness of and direction over
innumerable related lines. Let point (1) be in the heart as a point of
light. Lines are made up of invisible points of light.

(6) Let these lines extend farther and farther from and to you. Do
this as play, as a child. We are only grown-up children. Your feet
barely touch the earth. Let your attention, awareness, rise
effortlessly to the very top of the head, point (2)—the place of in-
telligence, in-telling. The secret of how to live and die is yours.
You are no longer the old you but rather an angelic being. So it
feels. But do not fly too high or too far. We need you to help others
to fly, to pass over ponderous troublings and stiff painings so lightly.

each in his mind cage
sticks out
arm
leg

Dear Bill,   [*1968*]

Readers Digest wrote up W. P. Knowles on breath three times since 1952. Once in 1966. I bought his course for $16 in USA and interviewed him in London. He has sold 100,000 persons his method over the years. It is a good one. It derives from yoga, much simplified though he says it comes from a Zoroastrian doctor Hanish who I think lifted it from yoga as they all do.

But his *results* come from nonviolence breathing and, I say, from: a few breaths set a pattern for many others. His course is a long series of exercises graduating in deeper breathing. Unless one pays for it and gets it weekly one misses doing it. I do not agree with all this and have said my way in an article. It is the only solution to yoga forced breathing I ever have discovered and believe it is of immense value as I think it actually lengthens the entire breath habit and so for the first time gives a way to direct otherwise sporadic nerve impulses.

This is a most important communication to you. It actually gives a method of regeneration. This has been lost in yoga because gentle guidance was lost and because yoga was only for the few, not the many.

Dear Bill,   [*1970*]

It is been my joy to receive my old friend Takeo Omori on his way back to Japan from a USA trip. He is the inventor and company founder, manufacturing machines he invents for packaging etc. with 100 employees.

Omori-san has also invented an instant zen without zen, a way to get IN our other world by a progressive relaxation method.

It is very simple.   It works.   It will better one's life.

The reason I write this is that you suggest it in a recent letter to me saying the way to avoid the bad air may be in. Omori thinks so. Sometimes in bad air, with wife problems, with food etc. he dismisses them all with his practice. We have had far too many *worded* ways. And clubbings.

Dear Bill,   [*1966*]

Buckminster Fuller is my friend. This started by my sending him a 10 or 20 dollar bill after reading your article on him years ago (now he is world noted) to support his ideas. He returned it.

Spent some time with him in Boulder last year. I think he is set. He and I are opposites. He wants results, places for people to dwell in. He alone is modern in providing such shelters.

But who shall make the people to live in them? Or shape?

Bucky has become quite stiff in his movements. He is sacrificing himself for his ideas, the best, but why sacrifice so ardently? Christian puritan slant.

I am very well! But if I had any disease I would simply go to Ann Wigmore in Boston. Have started her grass juice and find she is right on it (from my experience). I sleep on the floor on 4" foam.

Dear Bill,   [*1976*]

All the energy that got us to the moon is now focused on getting us to live better and this even more than now will lead us far from the primitive way. Ex-citing!

I heard Bucky give a talk last year and met him again in hotel in Victoria. He simply beamed love, a great heart; but I had to rebuke him for stealing an hour of waiting time from 2,000 in audience AND FOR BEING SO STIFF.

I wrote him things to do to loosen up so live longer but don't know if he will obey me.

Flexive = young   stiff = old   and we choose degrees of either.

walking through
the forest
rearranging
the trees

napa

Let

breath
breathe

then ————

the
great
breath

A SINGLE BREATH

Breath habits, like any other habits, affect us. What is that breath that may free us spiritually and materially? Centuries ago yoga taught the use of purified breath to liberate consciousness. Egyptians knew a sun-breath, both revealing and concealing it in their statues. Buddha conquered Hindustan with a breath of love. Ghandi earned Indian independence with a few effective words on breath, "Go home, we don't want you here." Islam rose as a world religion as their saints accomplished yogic miracles with a divine breath. The Chinese magnificently explored the day-night electro-magnetic breath of nature in human nature. Japanese archers, African hunters, American Indian dancers, and in fact anyone who ever perfected a skill, related it to breathing techniques.

What is that breath — that single breath — that may free us spiritually and materially? We might call it the immanent instant breath of God. Surely it is no breath-device man has practiced. How do we come to it? By grace — humbly, honestly, simply by receiving, in faith. By unifying a single in- and out-breath. Faith is felt and breathed more than thought.

Receptive to God — expressive to man/ Completely passive inbreathing — thankfully outbreathing/ Release of all heart tensions, all I-ness, when inbreathing — joyous action with outbreaths/ Doing and being no-thing inbreathing — being yourself and no one else outbreathing, thus joining prayer and power. These are the ways *into* but are not the blessing itself.

Often by civilized mannerisms our breath may have become reversed without our being aware of it. Then we are fighting ourselves, and self-violence is never personal freedom. Restrictions on inbreaths cramp the heart and bloodflow. They probably shorten our life — at the very least have us uneasy, miserable, egocentric. When we do not act in rhythm with outbreaths, our power is sapped. We make sounds on outbreaths. We exert, or should exert, on outbreaths. A woodchopper chops on outbreaths. Hard work coordinated with outbreathing becomes tireless. Try it.

We breathe in and out 22,000 times each 24 hours. Our cells as expectant children anticipate organic guidance. We need not breathe anger or petulance through them for these are only constrictions. No constrictions is sheer joy Mind and muscle, feeling and breathing and moving are truly unseparate through us. We divide them unnecessarily and set them against one another. Just be and breathe your natural self. Tensions against yourself are unnatural. Free them in whatever you are doing.

And each day, at least for a few breaths, inbreathe the *infinite presence*. This is so easy it seems unbelievable — that a single breath may have us whole.

To the perfect
the imperfect appears perfect.
To the imperfect
even the perfect seems imperfect.

Never breath.
Let breath breathe.
Let breath pause.

Never breathe out,
forcing willfully.
Force knowingly.

Let breath breathe in,
into rhythms of great nature,
ours, more than ours.
To let is to will too, lovingly.

Let breath pause:
Sit comfortably, eyes closed or near closed.
Courageously let breath breathe 20 breaths
and watch the 21st out-in
and let the 22nd pause —
recharging,
rejuvenating.

(It will, Let it. This is the way to grow younger as well as older, the way to shine as light. Outbreath, the way out, of lightness — inbreath the way in, of lightness — pause — the lightness.)

EXERCISE YES EXERCISE NO
paul reps

[This is an early version of an article later published in SQUARE SUN SQUARE MOON.]

Exercise yes exercise no. Animals never exercise.

They keep moving. They move and rest move and rest move and rest. When they get out of breath it is to save their life. They go around naked, eat unfired food when wild, sleep outdoors. They never die. They return to animal.

Man never dies. He experiences something he names death but he cannot conceive I am not. Self speaks **I AM** through all nature, the Big Self. The small self is already dead.

By airplane two hours north of Stockholm in Sweden and an hour of driving into the forest brings me to the finest athletic training establishment perhaps in the world, the only one with spring moss. Here at Valadalens , the name of a no-town, I meet Gosta Olander, world famous for having trained more champion athletes than anyone. He has spent 35 years in the building of these dwellings, athletic fields, skating rinks, ski jump and a fine mountain hotel with the healthiest young patrons. I ask him his secret. He does not say. He shows me.

He takes me to an 800 metre grey sand beach edging a lake. You run a few miles in this soft sand to strengthen your feet and legs. Then you jog over to the spring moss and run on it barefoot. Each step springs you up, so soft and pillowy is the turf. It helps inject a flexive response through your musculature. It is like running on a mattress only better.

Then you continue running on one of the many narrow mountain paths made by the Lapps with their reindeer herds, narrow so you run in a straight line and up and downhill for stamina.

Nature is speaking Olander's secret. No wonder all manner of athletes are learning from him. The air is charged with win. What is the secret?

Keep moving. Come out of doors. Learn from the animals. Go to bed with the birds. Get into the game of life. Eat live foods to build live cells. Welcome rain, thank sun, keep supple, sense, move.

The strength, endurance and speed Olander evokes in others are of nature. He only channels the big message into the champions, merely human champions winning at artificed games and remembering it the rest of their lives. But they get a rich reward. They live longer and better and cleaner for having drawn from nature, their nature.

Come in the *batsdu* , the Finnish sauna, where in the dry hot rooms your billion pores let go and out come the poisons and you feel fresher for a week. When you are done pouring sweat you jump into the cold pool, in winter into the snow — if you can get in his place packed with skiers.

Three miles up that mountain is a lake full of fish. Run there. Spring. Save *your* life. All you have to do is take to the forest, forget style and the paraphernalia of anti-you.

All you have to do is to keep flexive, supple. Any cat can teach you this. Move smooth. Move and rest. Move all through, when resting really rest through every cell. Don't listen to others, don't be restless for amusements.

Next you return to the spring moss for release.

It takes only two or three weeks of this for you to become a champion. You take a plunge in the cold pool and are ready for superb Swedish food, health itself. What buttermilk and applesauce!

You are doing this at an altitude of 1500 feet that produces more red blood cells immediately. In the pure mountain air, in an athlete's environment of no smoking, no drinking, no indulging, no idle talk, no cars, no sidewalks, no stores and everyone with one intent.

Next you study the animals in a large zoo who teach you movement. The Himalayan bears show you how to move from center; the foxes — alertness; the wolverines — tirelessness; the deer — sensitivity; the flamingos — how to step; the crow — observation. No animal is so foolish as to define such qualities. Animal lives them as they live him. The ego is man's invention.

You study the Lapps in wigwam houses with turf sides and boughs for floor, men strong as forest trees, always outdoors.

And when you move don't tighten your neck. Loosen those wrists. Don't make faces. Run ahead of yourself. Loosen that neck.

It's late morning 5 A.M. The big bear opens one eye and looks at me. He uncurls, gives a tremendous yawn, curls up again, breathes a long outbreath into his fur and goes to sleep. The best sleep is after waking. The best waking is early. There's something in the air. The owl as large as a small barrel opens an unblinking eye. He eyes everything he needs to see.

What is our mother nature but this shrub, this weed, this you *in relation* to this me, in infinite surprise relations. Pardon these stiff words for the adventure.

You can't run in heels, in high heels. You really can't. You can follow behind another's style for a while. Here young women are as athletically inclined as men. What good is a construction that can't run? You can't be sick and run.

Run is only to run, 10 more steps each day. It costs nothing. To ever be sick is expensive business.

Heart is the mover. Whatever we think as mind only surfaces heart power. Animals move *with* heart. That's their big secret. We are animals too, sense-crippled but cunning.

A man does what he must. Olander was born to teach athletes, to bridge man and nature uniquely. But how about us? How about us cats?

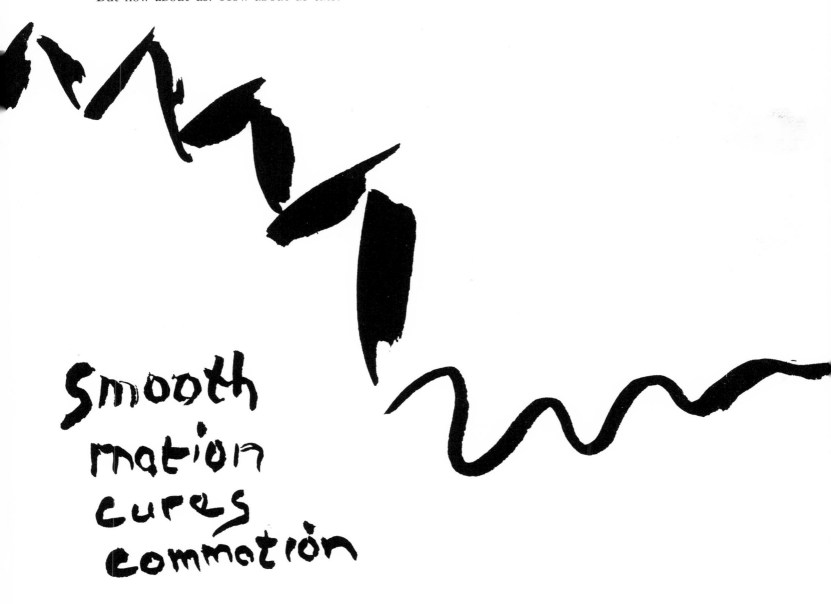

smooth
motion
cures
commotion

Dear Bill,   *[1963]*

Yoga says if you pull UP in middle you make for youth. This is I believe a fanning vertically of the diaphragm. Trampoline forces this fanning, soon makes my wind better, also reducing middle, so feels good. Splendid with a good teacher but must progress slowly. Gets to be more and more fun.

Walking upstairs is exercise, hence breath labor. It seems bouncing up and down on trampoline is similar labor, hidden by fun and challenge, so requires more oxygen so oxygenates blood so by this fanning wind gets better.

REPORT JUST TO YOU
who is reps just came from early coldish summery tomidsummer
in a day of 48 hours flying time from Hambugg Germany to Hong Kong
to be waamly welcomed by allmy chinese friends in this chinese inn
and a special dinner from Luu; the handreading expert of this world.
Igrabbed his right hand and read a tremendously long life in
his lifeline. Thispleased him because it was fun, surprise, and
touch. The whole day no one TOUCHES us; we wear clothes and a mind
to keep them away. If someone does all barriers are broken.We
are children playing.   They plan a poem exhibit in the big city HK
art gallery (please not art, red berries) under slogan for 65
WILD BIRD FLY BY that got the best gallery and many folks so
excited inGoteborg and then in Valadalens sweden; and then another
Kyoto exhibit is being planned I hear by friends. Poems everywhere
all free but the wild bird fly by he not even smile maybe he eagle
evern sparrow will do; driving a VW through Norway fjords for
fourth time how the birds swoop down and play fly with car surprise
a month in swedish forest at 2,000 feet plus running makes new man of
me; feel just fine: Formula: RUN 10 STEPS EACH DAY AND ADD ONE
EACH DAY. Am up to 300 now, tirelessly, no jolts; anyone can with
this method; swim stretches run tightens ligaments; runnershave a
secret joy they cannot tell. It comes from self discipline
gradually with considerate motion. Swim stretches. Run tightens
ligaments and vibrates unheard music in the runner.

Bill   *[1965]*

When I fail it takes a little longer. See my letter failed to tempt you to RUN 10 EACH DAY and add one,,, maybe i should say prance. You only refer to when you *were* a runner. This is not the point. Why not learn to run to run, not to win. You walk to walk. That's what makes it fun, né ? ZZZah!

dear kids,

    here I am again, they say for the 15th spring in norway
and hi! how are you, bill? it takes me a week or more
to condition after an air trip.

    here is my great discovery   A COLD PLUNGE
last year it felt so cold I didn't go in but this year
i PLUNGED IN and started to swim.

    since my mind I discover can only hold one
thing at a time, as soon as I plunged I forgot the
cold entirely in the swim   they say the pool
is heated but the shock to bones is very fine
I swum each day in a huge pool in victoria
but never felt such effect   so I say   after
hot or even before a cold shower   try it
plunge is better.

the
runner

```
BILL   The winter number of AF has the spirit
of reps all thru, one I never could appreciate,
indescribably bright. This issue predicts a BIG
future for USA indeed. You sure are doing your
stuff. And Lully cover is excellent too, mag.
cover sexy both front and back. Gals inside
all have their legs apart. Other night 2,000
teen-age kids busted up stores, autos, every
thing in sight in Hollywood strip protesting
agains the curfew imposed on them by police to
protect night joints for youth LSD customers.
So we have a revolution inside a revolution.
Police found an Arizona boy laughing, so
joyous who had shot 5 girls dead as they lay
on the floor.  I am a mountain man.       .
```

GREAT SNOW

also on top of mt I live under, Moana Kea
once heavy with white snow

seeing snow symbolizes death to japanese (white)
and purity to white skinners
and oneness to philosophers
and warmth to small animals

Dear Bill,   [1961]

Your retainer of world reporter for AF check came the day I was leaving, showering me with expense money and your blessings.

Tahiti: Stuart Hotel, eat at Waikiki and an upstairs French restaurant, the code, boat to North part, Cook, off Morea, 9 AM on a good day, hire car around island, 1 day is the schedule. But tourists miss it, being taken to $10 a day hotels and sold tours.

Tahiti has two main exports, moral depravity and tourism, both just beginning.   Something starting like that might do you a page article, should you wish it with some (of your) Tahiti sketchings.

Love (the exploration of space) opposites indulgence and perhaps this place more than any other on earth never even heard of marriage customs; lush island, small population; lawlessness, bone structure in decay from sugar. What grapefruit!!

Sit down, breathe, cool sea air at oceanfront, muggy a few blocks back/ nature starts to speak in you/ thus assimilation begins. But come in cool season here.

My adventure: Motorbike, 1st I was ever on/ should lead to Vespa/ a splendid way to travel, wind in face where motor cars are not overthick. Lots of fun. No gas fumes here, hurrah.

Dear Bill,   [1962]

In 1952 all the chorus girls had fat thighs. Now fat thighs are unseen. Also now Japanese minds are changing and due to new teaching methods in schools they are learning English much faster. This means they have a kind of thrill to try to speak it so when they see a foreigner they delight. This delight is very sweet and innocent. It comes to me wherever I go in Japan. So simply walking down any street becomes a surprising adventure. My few speaking words make it possible for me to travel alone too.

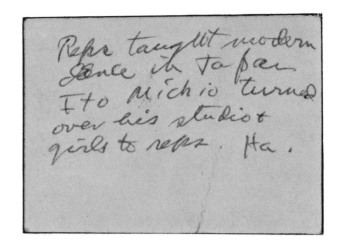

Reps taught modern dance in Japan Ito Michio turned over his studio & girls to reps. Ha.

Dear Bill,   [1969]

Yucatan, bill, is very light and bright so be sure and have dark glasses along; Mexico I have been many times, but here be sure to have apple cider vinegar, a spoonful in a glass of water will purify the water and stop running bowels overnight.

I almost forgot about Morocco   why not!
The children of the world are our best places to visit and there they are in Mexico, too cold in New Mexico now; I don't say be afraid but be wise and stock up food water heat against emergent emergencies and have a VW ready to decamp in or decorate the Cadillac lavishly as AF is always lavish in decorations.

Dear Bill.   [1967]

Everything comes to us we deserve and only what we deserve. From meeting a man who has just come from Agadir, S. Morocco, I learn that Club Mediterranee, Agadir, is THE place to go in Morocco. I shall go there as press reps for *American Fabrics Magazine*. You should go too. Also from there you can take a 6 day trip through the desert, spending enroute 3 days in Marrakesh.

This will be a much better adventure for you to look forward to. You should pay for your entire stay to the Club Mediterranee, N.Y.C., as you get a far better money exchange than in Morocco.

This letter so far has no point. Now we come to the point. Rothschild has established these clubs to give some meaning to people who go places. It is an idea contraverting the bankrupt American idea of cement cells over the world for tourists unhappy in or out of them or themselves. No doubt you know about this Club idea already so will not detail it. But a new idea is always something . . .

Dear Bill,   *[1962]*

It was terrifically hot in Hongkong. They gave me two huge Chinese dinners, all Chinese present admiring the poems. In a day I was in Frankfurt, and the next day got my VW Camper in Hamburg and the next day in Denmark. Am presently living in Molde, Norway in the heart of the fjord country.

Oh the pure wined air, the water, the cheese and raspberries and blue eyes. On this my third trip I begin to understand what is going on in **BLUE EYED PERSONS** that brown eyes miss; namely the bewined air of the forests and streams. Norway folk are sparce drinkers but here everyone is drunk on this air and water. It is just another example of nature making man. I must say the fjord country is the most beautiful place on earth; am saying it in an article.

BROWN EYES   emotive, hot, extravagant
BLUE EYES   cold, cool, exact, bewildered, simple, pure but by the way this war between blue and brown went on for centuries; now the english are surrendering fast. Let us turn to **GREEN** eyes next.

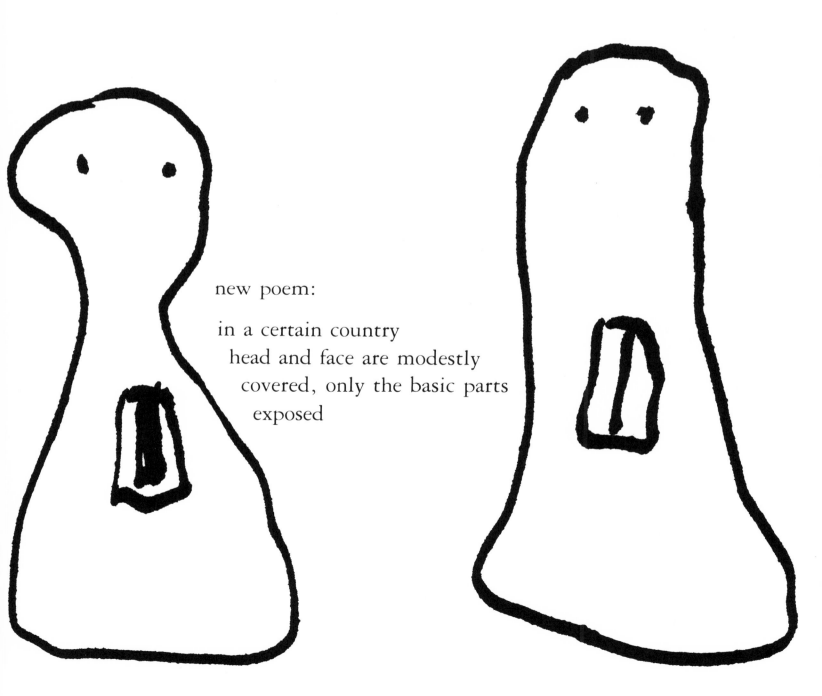

new poem:

in a certain country
   head and face are modestly
     covered, only the basic parts
      exposed

reps box 11, hilo
7 Oct 64

Dear Bill,

THANK YOU
THANK YOU
THANK YOU for the big $100 for your travelling press
                              repsresentative.

Now I sent you Isometrics for the fun of it
but that book (there are others that dont) stressed held-in breath
and this stems from Yoga, the opposite of Moslem held-out
and in contradistiction to reps never breathe breath.

I lost lost your letter. It dropped out of my back pocket
in a Samurai movie when it got bloodiest
but I phoned the theater and they found it!
           COMING INTO MINDLESSNESS IS JUST GREAT

With such a title
to an article
it is almost immortal
I didn t want to alter the content but to fortify it
if you write it. I am always asking readers to look over
my stuff, and that is all I meant in re editing yours.
I always get good suggests too from anyone.
We should not change an original writing but sometimes
slight muddiness can be helped.
For example: a woman writes me:(about her yoga)

                I meditate in divine JOY.
                May same be released in you
             as your permanent companion and reality.

I sent her a postcard saying: Are you a Baptist?
What do you mean by divine? Could some other word
make it clearer?

That's all. Then she has to stew about that.

But I am going to send her a follow-up postcard asking:
Dont you think a sentence gains power with a one word
impact rather than a this and that one?
For example: Could one word work better than
your "companion and reality" ?

Every time I cut out saying two things instead of one _in one sentence_
I add force and import to what is said, if there is such
in anything we say.
This is example of reps editing.

An expert reader has read my 77 (my masterpeace) 5 times
each time I get special suggests from her on it.
It is a pre-book. No doubt after it appears there will
be no more need for books.   There are a thousand orchids
growing in my front yard, along the road many flowers of all colors
and trees. I had an egg sandwich on rye for dinner. Swam in
the ocean with a big dog. Got a letter from a woman I met in 59
on the beach who wants names of my books. I cant recall her
but can, the books. THANKS AGAIN!!!!!   _reps ing_

Screen of Love

Coming from the vast stone Catholic monastery of Montserrat in Spain in my Volkswagen, the little German car most fun to drive, I whizzed downhill in southern France. Past a sign reading N9 Le Boulon 19 St. Jean de l'abre 5, I looked back to see, as in a flash of light, a thin straight woman with a face shining like a star.

As I passed her she smiled at me, saying something I did not understand. She was dressed in white and brown robes of some religious order. She was holding in her right hand the reins of a big grey burro.

Only rarely have I seen such radiance in human form. A moment earlier or later, a turn of the head another way, and I might have missed her.

"Drive on," something within me said, "and do not diminish such a view of nature by meeting her."

Several miles farther on, I stopped to eat some roadside grapes for it was September. After the grapes, since the car and I were wanderers, it turned around of itself, and started back to see if I had seen what I had seen.

She was on the highway now. I drove up to her and stopped. At once she shook hands with me in a wholly free and friendly way. "Très jolie," she exclaimed about the car, the sunny day, our meeting, or something she was feeling.

We tried to talk but she could hardly understand my garbled Spanish, French and English. She was in the radiance I had glimpsed when passing her. We exchanged addresses.

Then she invited me to her cloister. Who was there? A Father and six nuns. Her name was Sister Elizabeth, but I called her Saint Elizabeth.

Up the side road we started. I in the little car and
(please turn)

she on her big burro. Sometimes driving ahead, I would wait for the sound of the burro-bells as she came joyously in sight. I found some paper-wrapped sugar lumps in the car and fed them to the burro.

The road branched off into a rocky gulley and later was hidden by huge blackberry brambles. Farther on it became so steep that I decided to walk.

Elizabeth and the portly Father were awaiting me. They received me with welcome as warm as if I had been a friend for years. Elizabeth disappeared into one of the buildings.

Would I visit the chapel? Of course. It was a small, unpainted wooden room named for St. Paul. There was a hidden wing for the women to use for worship.

Would I meet the Mother Superior? Of course. We went into another small room, one side of which was covered with a wire screen with quarter-inch openings. Behind this screen the Mother appeared with Elizabeth and another sister. Each was like a bubbling spring.

How strange — meeting such humans behind wire netting, much as I had talked with prisoners in the United States. But on which side was the prison? Were they on the inside or the rest of us on the outside the real prisoners?

What was my name? Where was I going? What was my religion?

"This stone floor, these walls take on your love," I told them. "And the tree coming in through the window, and the burro. My religion is your love."

✶ ✶ ✶

The women had built the cloister with their own hands. The food they ate, the simple wooden crosses they wore, every detail was a product of their effort in this semi-desert country, quite like our California desert.

Would I eat something? I ate a leaf off the tree, but this they felt was not enough. The Father led me to a small dining alcove where, through an opening in the wall, appeared luscious green figs, yellow scrambled eggs with herbs, green string beans, red tomatoes — a feast such as I had not tasted in eleven countries.

The Father told me he always ate alone, and that he would be serving me himself, were he not blind. I had not noticed his eyes. "You are not blind. I am blind," I replied, "the people of the world whose minds and hearts are shut *are* blind, not you."

After I had eaten, we met again for coffee in the room with the screen. Would I return? What were my plans? I would never leave this place!

"We are one," they told me — just as Mirak Shah, the Kashmir Pir had exclaimed near the Shalimar gardens — just as the Sufi, Inayat Khan, had indicated in his invocation: Toward the *One,* the perfection of love, harmony and beauty.

"You will be in our prayers," the Mother and Father said. I thanked them for words so pure, for the needs of the pure have ways of being filled.

The Mother gave me a tiny image that had brought much good to others she said. Afterward I buried it in the earth whose living presence might transmit its wishes to mankind. But just in case, I recovered it and have it with me as a kind of receiver for their love.

Elizabeth was quite as free on one side of the screen as on the other. A printed slip she gave me said they were associated gloriously and consumed in a joyous holocaust of love of God, through penance, petition, prayer, contemplation and silence.

What is the source of their spirit, this inner light that so transforms humans? Had such come to them because of their humbleness and sincerity, because they are drinking pure water, working in clear air, observing long hours of self-discipline including two hours twice a day of silence?

Why did I feel that love, and even more, from the burro? Why had I felt the burro telling Elizabeth, as she urged him on up the road to the cloister, "Hurry to receive this man? Have you not already received each other?"

St. Elizabeth had given me her address as Monastère Ermita Maire, Val de l'Albere par Le Perthus, Pyrénées Orientales, France. Although I shall send them something for their building fund, they are to me the richest persons in Europe.

✶ ✶ ✶

"Au revoir, mes enfants, je vous aime." I drove the car down the loose rocks to turn it around in their garden. As I started up the burro pushed his head and shoulders in one window to keep me from going. He knew, better than I, as I discovered later, that there was one more lump of sugar remaining in that car.

31 Oct 54

Dear Bill,

      You should drop a note to Saint Elizabeth
saying you are considering publishing Reps story
and would she send you any snapshots of herself and
burro and of monastery,

      as Reps has written requesting her to do in
another letter in English.

Paul reps

      This note should be translated in French as
they do not read English and it may take them a long
time to get my request translated. My Ms and request to them
was not airmail either.

ON FIRE
means clarly wholly devoted to mankind's good
purposively expressed and articulated,
the privilege of americans as world leaders
and publishers as america's leaders—
You have a great mission, my friend and a
body and responsiveness to accomplish it
Let me help you,

Dear Bill, [1964]

Send me check for $1,000. I will equal amount. We are building the "poem house" supervised by Yoshioka, architect. It will cost $2000 or less but we will have a gem place.

On leased land of friend of some years, Omori, owner of a company, an inventor of machineries; when he saw our plans offered me free any of 3 of his country places. 500 *tsubo* (1000 mats) land; he will build house on concurrent or before with ours, but no connection, but Yoshioka supervises his house and ours. I also will duplicate this project in Hilo, Hawaii.

Dear Bill, [1965]

The house is up, a 12 x 32 redwood rectangle looking tall and small in that 2 acre fenced-in piece of land overlooking the sea that you saw at such a disadvantage in the rain. It rains much less there in Paauilo than in Hilo.

The point of it is that it has a plastic roof like enclosed so the thing is a house of light, added to by a big tipped out window and aluminum sliding doors and other windows. We can call it our poem house all right; everyone reacts to it, farmers and all, with a kind of delight wonder. The tall trees shade it from the sun too. I move in tomorrow. It was cut in the shop, each piece of wood, and put up by 5 expert Japanese carpenters, a team, in 3 days. The plumber took 1 day, the electrician the same 1 day, the cesspool man 3 days, that's all. The earth goes down 9 feet of rockless rich soil, then 4 feet of fine black pulvarized earth, very old volcanic, then some small rocks, this soil almost unheard of here. The cattle, they say, grow better in this area than any other. It is the oldest geologically and earthquake extinct, 1900 feet altitude, the same as at Valadalens, Sweden. It is yours to use and enjoy. Do so!!

The carpenters came from Hilo. Each day thru rain. When they got there they had no rain at all. The electric co. heads became my friends and made some special quick concessions. It all went magically well. I did not work on it myself tho am a housebuilder too, 4.

REPS POEM HOUSE
A REALITY

That fellow now named reps (he says: "I don't know my name tomorrow") has bought a fenced in, squared, on road, with water and lights and telephone (he won't have) 1900 foot elevation, overlooking the blue Pacific, wind-sheltered yet wafted, fertile, gently rolling, surrounded on 3 sides with huge eucalyptus, a veritable cathedral, cool, cloud-sunny, sublime, almost on private road, always growable for vegetables, horse and cow grazing if gate open, hordes of berries vivee over top hill, lush, verdant, hunk of land for $3000 for the USA poem house, as close as anyone should get to the mainland, never winter, never too hot, brisk, air-purified by altitude and eucalyptus, and now what do we do next, who knows   banzai   beginning.

There are a thousand small wild orchids in my front yard. My big picture window looks to the sea a block away whose roar sings in my ears. Green trees with red blossoms, white blossoms, bushes so big they take over the trees, ripening bananas in the yard, papaya trees, purple flowers out my bathroom window, and when I walk to swim a lavish procession of flowering.

It never gets cold or hot and when it rains it stops in such a short time so I come out from under a palm and because of the rain it is ever green.

There are a hundred sheltered swim coves inside the breakers, each one the most beautiful place in this paradise. A big show comes on each sundown when the skies are painted variously. I charge $10 just to sit on my front porch and see it. No one ever pays, they can see it from everywhere. The cloud and sun view from the control tower at the airport is something to see, where my friends instruct the incoming planes. I eat about six papayas a day at 4¢ a pound. No traffic. No telephone. I am 50 feet from sea level and tidal wave, directly in path of last volcanic lava flow, feel quakes sometimes, swim a swift river and jump on return into its waterfall that carries me clear across it in a minute.

Life must be risked to counteract all this beauty.

and please send two dozen windows

among these mountains minds appear

Dear Paul   [*1962*]

By way of passing—I was hit over the head a few weeks ago by a large branch, while I was working in the forest; and I had to have quite an operation on my skull. My head is now shaven and I look very much like some of the priests we saw in Japan—really well-disguised.

Bill

Dear Bill,

I am shocked to hear you were hit by nature on your head. Please send me a photo of yourself to prove it.

I hope the operation did not remove part of the skull.

We are everyday subject to small shocks. This was a huge one. If I could get such a shock I might cancel the old reps entirely, start afresh.

The closest I can come to this so far is 5 Tibetan rites to grow younger. They seem to work, are much simpler and more balancing than Hindu Yoga.

Try for balancing, ambidextrous positioning and moving while recuperating, 5 minutes each hour exactly.

We see, I believe, with one or the other eye; hear with one ear. If we can get eyes centered the phenomenal world bother cuts out. This is what the tree was trying to do for you.

In Japan sometimes woodchoppers ask a tree's forgiveness before chopping.
It might be well.

Get well!!

Paul Reps

direct
experience

Dear Bill,   [*1973*]

You haven't long to live,
not over 100 years which is as a day.
Why not give yourself a new life
into nature and surrender to air
and light instead of to the business
you have done so well?

Why not send a notice: **ON VACATION**,
and simply stop the magazine
until vacation is over,
which might be in 5 years.

Do not let the magazine become a money drain.
Act decisively, sharply and be
wonderful
YOU

Dear Bill,   [*1968*]

you are the publisher of magazines breathing the metallic air
of new york and keeping busy . . .

            IF   and I disbelieve it
                      you are in a great sweat because
                      of different pressures
                      you are not acting like a potato

if you give me your original full christened name and a bit of
detail on the kind of sweat, I can give you a palliative.

Dear Bill,   [*1977*]

Just received your latest *American Fabrics Magazine*.   Man, what a fine issue!   A swell job!   But who is doing this?   You?   Then does this mean you die soon because man must get his feet onto earth to survive and this must keep your feet off earth to do it?

Also you may be the enemy of humanity because you are advocating artificial fabrics which are death-inviting because they cut off the sun rays and suns of suns rays our body needs.

Test this True? untrue? Prove it . . .

Your idea of making your wife work is splendid after all what are wives to do but w

dear bill,   [*1967*]

WOMEN DON'T SMELL ANY MORE

the reason you can't smell them is that their pores are clogged up with soap, their food is pap, they never touch the earth or sweat, and light cannot get at them because it is deflected with stones or invented metallics in their garments.

please let me know at once where i can buy a natural fabric cloth for my wearing.

also let me know if your wool advertising is for wool with its threads treated, which of course means a step towards sickness, not health.

in defense of my life and health i ask you for this information.

i bought the last pair of woolen socks in germany.

*standing
on earth
under
sky*

dear bill,   [*1968*]

   I like to report to you when I feel sick and well. I report that I am only beginning to recover in my raw tubes from breathing the New York City air for 10 days. I know you will respond with love to my confessed feeling. You are the expansive open man who *LOVES*.

        but
        you need air
        you must admit you breathe
        and need air   are you shrinking in there?

   if New York Central fails how many more will topple? will *AF* topple? when, as I read, the Pres of NY Stock Exchange complains that if they are not permitted to raise commission rates they will be out of business, I think maybe the gambling den, sucking in so many millions, is to be put out of business.

   Your NY is in you, you are reflecting it—This is POTATO INview. NY is strong because you are strong. I used to get the life sense from NYC that you do when I lived there.   not now.

husbands and kill them with dead overfired foods not to mention dead conversations.

dear bill: [1974]

1. In a recuperating body you need good simple natural food and I don't think you get it outside of France.

2. I see market as half way down and worse to come. Thus I question how *AF* can survive or any other mag. So I say drop it quick before it gets into you.

3. I wonder how NYC will be livable at all due to disruptions as bombing, atom bombing, power cut off etc. So say you are lucky to have your country home if you can defend it. And get there.

4. With this cheerful news I advise you of my arrival in Victoria and departure for Zen Center San Francisco for month of October.

dear bill,   [1973]

You mean well but are lost to interpret what you are doing when you zen or whirl with the dervishes. Being an in-tell-igent man you naturally want to survey the goings on from a wise position. But no one offers you this position so you propose to ask publicly about it from many others, but those others you would ask of are hard for you to find because you are going about it the hard way.

(The easy way would be to forget all your project and simply spend a year studying reps new manuscript GOO GURU completely treating this subject.)

You are also slowing down because of age and you must accept this and not try to run with the hysterical ones, mostly everyone.

For a change, take a look at yourself, and keep looking.

You also have a commitment to Marielle. And to *AF*.

However in the world of things you do have a skill to direct others as to how they may make a new magazine and this talent should be drawn upon by others.

Right now you are formulating how to have them do this. But you cannot write the mag as well as birth it. You need someone else to do that, that is, to draw a lot of minds. There may be a way to do it, but as yet you haven't found it. *UN Courier* has, for them, and they have done a good job. *Sports Illustrated* has for them and they are successful.

> **Zen has not done it for Zen**
> **and they are a closed group;**
> **that is, they do not recognize**
> **that all they are doing is sitting still.**
>
> **This is a stupendous failure to communicate that**
> **most persons are suffering from.**

The new world will remedy that.
It will all be life size on a wall.

Bill,   [*1972*]

Name me in your will. Give me Marielle.
You must be crazy to talk of starting a magazine
when *Life* can't make it   Or are you dreaming?
Or offer to buy *Life* and get some *AF* publicity.
On next *AF* cover say:

>   *AF* offers to buy *Life*.

then at bottom left say:

> but after this offer we learned that we can't buy *Life*, we have to
> live it. Naturally when living it we like to wear clothes alive. See
> inside for etc. etc.

I think your magazine idea came from a subconscious wish to promote your children
into a job. How about a little reorienting?

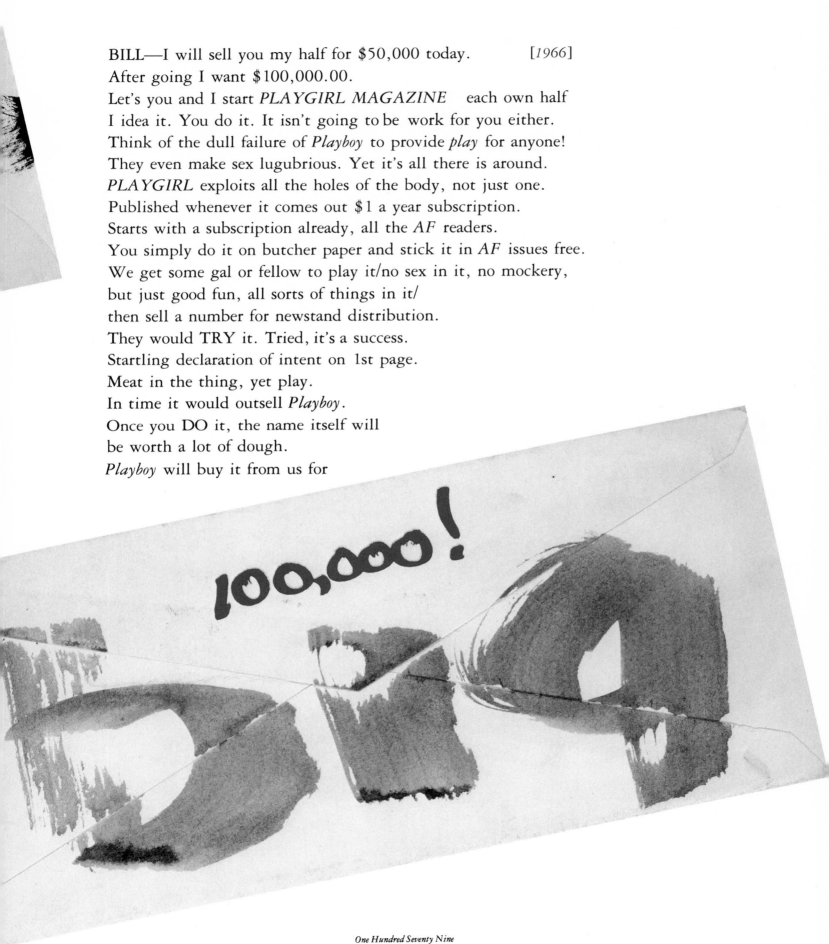

BILL—I will sell you my half for $50,000 today. [1966]
After going I want $100,000.00.
Let's you and I start *PLAYGIRL MAGAZINE* each own half
I idea it. You do it. It isn't going to be work for you either.
Think of the dull failure of *Playboy* to provide *play* for anyone!
They even make sex lugubrious. Yet it's all there is around.
PLAYGIRL exploits all the holes of the body, not just one.
Published whenever it comes out $1 a year subscription.
Starts with a subscription already, all the *AF* readers.
You simply do it on butcher paper and stick it in *AF* issues free.
We get some gal or fellow to play it/no sex in it, no mockery,
but just good fun, all sorts of things in it/
then sell a number for newstand distribution.
They would TRY it. Tried, it's a success.
Startling declaration of intent on 1st page.
Meat in the thing, yet play.
In time it would outsell *Playboy*.
Once you DO it, the name itself will
be worth a lot of dough.
Playboy will buy it from us for

100,000!

```
      Dear Bill,

      I infer subdued random music will be healing
      I infer slow rhythmic moving continuously
            to such music would be exercising
      I inger garlic and ginger tea would taste good
      I infer will + willing are need in equal doses
            willingness on receptive inbreath
      I see you as getting better
```

Dear Bill,   *[1971]*

I am amazed at your car accident story, one of superb health I should say and interest to carry thru it all. You must have been fortunate to get the right doctors too. This is another thing. And you so soon well. Unbelievable.

A research carried on for some 50 years by scientists worked on the fact that man has 23 and 28 day rhythms starting from birth, and when these rhythms make a certain pattern, they seem to have proved one is 7 or 8 times as accident-prone as other times. But I can't get this figured for you because you are not sure of your birth date.

Well, few have gone thru what you have, Bill, *AND SO SANELY*.

I wonder if the closed windows on the Cadillac could have blanked you out with foul gasses picked up from roadside, and held in car with no exit.

Dear Bill,   *[1972]*

Reading THE PRIMAL SCREAM and Janov's inquiry into things this thought comes to me:

> **You impress me as a very healthy specimen by inheritance. This means
> you must have had very virile parents. So then why couldn't those parents
> install a terrific feel block in you at an early age, something so strong as to
> give you an unconscious urge to break out of it; and this break
> exemplified by your willful smashup.**

Janov, who repudiates all psychotherapy, is on a live track it seems to me / read him.

Hi to Marielle herself, by the way. How fine she takes care of you so well. Why not longer trips, longer stays?

More love and feeling / you say. This implies more personal effusion.

But what if just more *FEEL*?

What if to be is to *feel* and all there is to do is to *FEEL*?

Perhaps love is like butter, but feel like the unseen vitamins in the food. Just a notion from the ocean.

Once in Hawaii you drove so fast back to Hilo I couldn't keep up with you. Fast driving = energy exuberance willful haste   good will   faster

There are an increasing lot of smashups these days, probably the basic natural food has gone out so brain loses timing control   better to go to France for food and into nature to give the cells the zest for taking up the food?

ON DEATH!

[From a talk in Boulder, Colorado 6/20/79]

Question: What do you think happens at death?
Do you think all the distractions are eliminated?

Reps: What do you think happens in life? So you're experiencing sitting here. So you die. So you experience dying. So you don't die, you go through an experience. Experience experiencing. So nothing happens at all, any more than what happens in life, I think. Life is a dying and we're conscious, unconscious, conscious, unconscious, so we're dying every second and we're being born every second. So that's the electromagnetic substance of life which is that way. Nothing whatever happens except you experience something. But what do you think happens to a person who dies under my instructions which you already received? He dies in life. So the whole thing is shaken off because you experience death, you're not afraid of it and you don't worry at all, you just go into your inner light. And then people who die say it's all light. This is a very common experience. It is actually all light if you don't die in fear. So if you want to die, just die in light. But if you jump out of an 18 story building are you going to die in light or not? Maybe. You might say: Oooooooooooooooo!

Question: What makes you keep coming back?

Reps: Coming back, what do you mean?

Question: After you die, why do we reincarnate? Maybe I should back up.
Do you believe in reincarnation?

Reps: How is that possible? It isn't possible. There's no possibility of reincarnation in light. It's too fast. No possibility of birth or death in light. It's too fast. It's all alive. So if your mother is sick in Paris and you get the word she may be dying you go into your subconscious and you say: Now mother, I'm talking with you because subconscious is all one and I see you getting real better, getting better and you're going to live. Like that. So you communicate with your mother in Paris through subconscious, see? But imagine what it is when you are communicating in light, far above that. So that's way beyond an idea that me as an ego in a human body will therefore incarnate again. Because we don't know about that. You might deserve to incarnate as a worm. Or the Buddhas or the Jesus people might go into the worst kind of incarnation: to save the world. So it may all be changed. Nobody knows what they're going to say next or do next so why belabor yourself with this stiff old idea of reincarnation?

You're not even incarnated, so how can you reincarnate it?

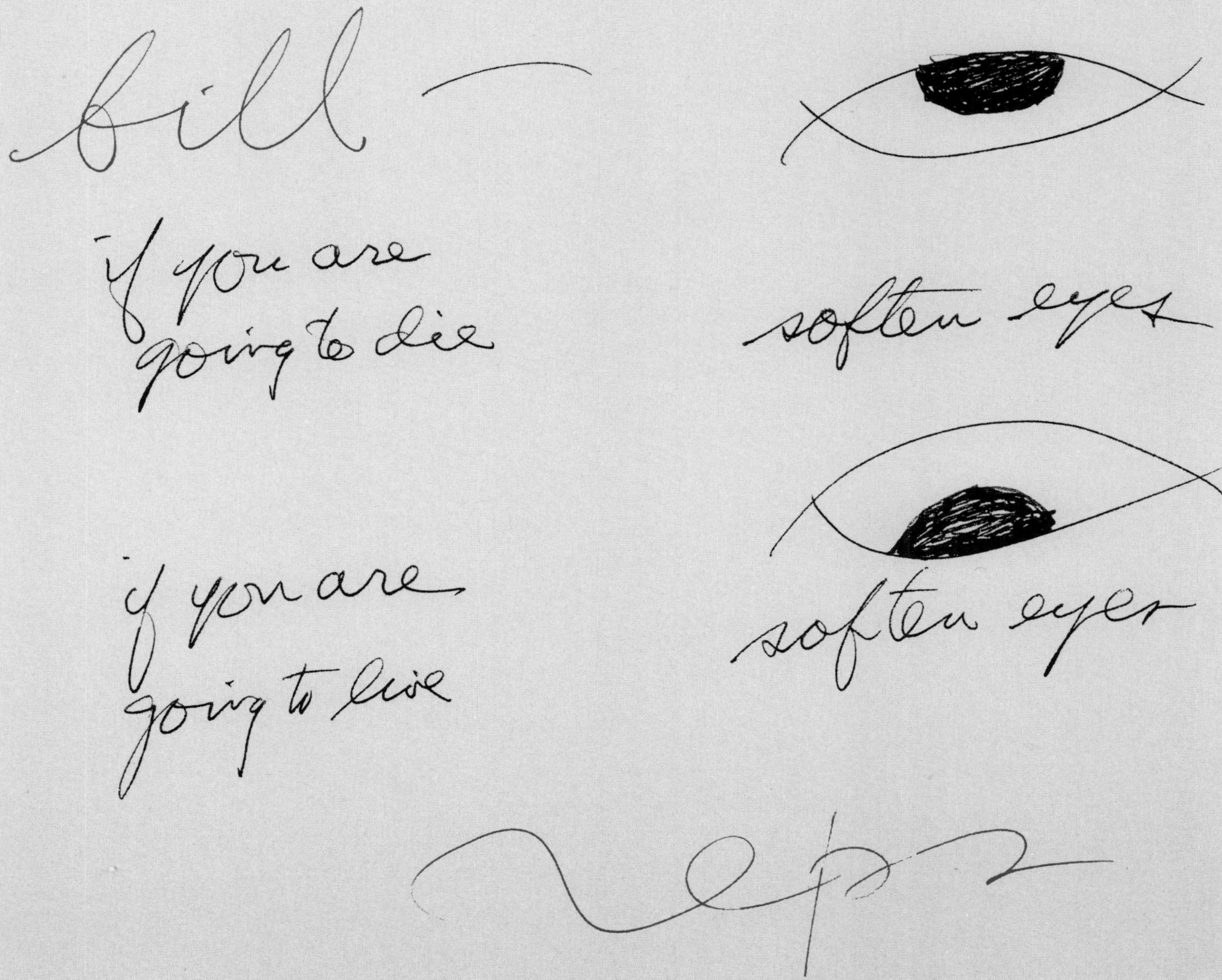

fill —

*if you are
going to die*

*if you are
going to live*

soften eyes

soften eyes

1939 — **MORE POWER TO YOU** (cloth) Preview Publications
1951 — **UNKNOT THE WORLD IN YOU** (paper) Sequoia University Press
1957 — **ZEN FLESH ZEN BONES** (cloth, slipcased) Charles Tuttle Co.
   consisting of:
     101 ZEN STORIES (Rider/McKay, 1939)
     THE GATELESS GATE (John Murray, 1934)
     10 BULLS (DeVorss, 1935)
     CENTERING (Gentry Magazine, 1955)
1958 — **KOMO HADAKA ARUKI** (NAKED ESSAYS BY A WANDERING FOREIGNER)
   [Published in Japan only; very sexy, says Reps.]
1959 — **ZEN TELEGRAMS** (cloth, slipcased) Tuttle
1960 — **BIG BATH** (paper) Liu Publishers
1961 — **GOLD/FISH SIGNATURES** (rice paper) Tuttle
1961 — **ZEN FLESH ZEN BONES** (paper) Doubleday & Co.
1962 — **ZEN TELEGRAMS** (paper) Tuttle
1964 — **PICTURE POEM PRIMER** (paper) Liu/American Fabrics
1965 — **UNWRINKLING PLAYS** (paper) Tuttle
1967 — **ASK A POTATO** (paper) American Fabrics
1967 — **SQUARE SUN SQUARE MOON** (paper) Tuttle
1969 — **GOLD/FISH SIGNATURES** (paper) Tuttle
1969 — **10 WAYS TO MEDITATE** (hardcover/mahogany boards) Walker/Weatherhill
1971 — **BE!** (paper) Walker/Weatherhill
1975 — **SIT IN** (paper) Zen Center Press
1978 — **JUICING** (paper) Doubleday

PAUL REPS: LETTERS TO A FRIEND/WRITINGS/DRAWINGS was edited and designed by Stillgate Publishers. This first edition is limited to 2500 copies. Printing by Halliday Lithograph. Color printing by New England Book Components. Japanese paper printing by Rich Lithograph. The gold paper was silkscreened by Simon Chalfoun and the silk tissue paper was silkscreened by Jane Collister. Binding by Robert Burlen & Sons.

The type was set in various sizes of Garamond. The lettering on the cover, title page and chapter title pages is a hand-lettered version of Lydian. The text paper is Mohawk Superfine Softwhite. Several varieties of Japanese paper were used—Moriki, Moriki Red, Teachest Gold and Silk Tissue. All of the papers in this book are acid-free, thereby guaranteed not to yellow or deteriorate over hundreds of years.

touch
this
to
come
down

JAN 1 4 1986